PYTHON PROGRAMMING FOR BEGINNERS

A Step-by-Step Guide to Learn one of the Most Popular and Easy Programming Languages. Learn Basic Python Coding Fast with Examples and Tips

Julian James McKinnon

© Copyright 2020 by Julian James McKinnon
All rights reserved.

The material contained herein is presented with the intent of furnishing pertinent and relevant information and knowledge on the topic with the sole purpose of providing entertainment.

The author should thus not be considered an expert on the topic in this material despite any claims to such expertise, first-hand knowledge, and any other reasonable claim to specific knowledge on the material contained herein.

The information presented in this work has been researched to ensure its reasonable accuracy and validity.

Nevertheless, it is advisable to consult with a duly licensed professional in the area pertaining to this topic, or any other covered in this book, in order to ensure the quality and validity of the advice and/or techniques contained in this material.

This is a legally binding statement as deemed so by the Committee of Publishers Association and the American Bar Association in the United States.

Any reproduction, transmission, copying, or otherwise duplication of the material contained in this work are in violation of current copyright legislation.

No physical or digital copies of this work, both total and partial, may not be done without the Publisher's express written consent. All additional rights are reserved by the publisher of this work.

The data, facts, and description of events forthwith shall be considered as accurate unless the work is deemed to be a work of fiction.

In any event, the Publisher is exempt of responsibility for any use of the information contained in the present work on the part of the user.

The author and publisher may not be deemed liable, under any circumstances, for the events resulting from the observance of the advice, tips, techniques and any other contents presented herein.

Given the informational and entertainment nature of the content presented in this work, there is no guarantee as to the quality and validity of the information.

As such, the contents of this work are deemed as universal.

No use of copyrighted material is used in this work.

Any references to other trademarks are done so under fair use and by no means represent an endorsement of such trademarks or their holder.

Table of Contents

Introduction 11

The Parts You Should Know about the Python Code 11

Getting That Environment Set Up 15

Chapter 1. Basic Background of Python 21

What Is Python? 25

Why Python? 25

Installing Python 32

Using a Text Editor 34

Using an IDE 35

Your First Program 36

Code Comments and Your Program 39

Chapter 2. Data Types in Python 43

Strings 43

Numeric Data Type 48

Booleans 49

List 50

Variables 51

User-Input Values 62

Chapter 3. Operators - The Types and Their Uses 67

The Types 67

The Operator Precedence 78

The Logical Operators 78

Chapter 4. Loops and Functions 86

LOOPS 86

Nested if Statements in Python 96

For Loop in Python 97

Range() Function in Python 99

Using for Loop with Else 100

While Loop in Python 101

Using While Loop with Else 102

Python's Break and Continue 103

Continue Statement in Python 104

Pass Statement in Python 106

Functions in Python 107

Calling a Function in Python 108

Docstring 109

Python Function Return Statement 110

Random Function in Python 110

Iterators 111

Manually Iterating Through Items in Python 112

Explaining the Loop 113

Creating Custom Iterator in Python 113

Infinite Iterators 115

Closure Function in Python 116

Projects - Implementing Simple Calculator in Python 119

Chapter 5. Exception Handling 122

What Is Exception Handling? 122

Handling the Zero Division Error Exception 122

Using Try-Except Blocks 125

Reading an Exception Error Trace Back 129

Using Exceptions to Prevent Crashes 131

The Else Block 134

Failing Silently 138

Handling the File Not Found Exception Error 139

Checking If File Exists 139

Try and Except 140

Creating a New File 142

Chapter 6. Variable Scope and Lifetime in Python Functions 143

Function Types 144

Keywords Arguments in Python 146

Arbitrary Arguments 147

Recursion in Python 148

Python Anonymous Function 149

Python's Global, Local and Nonlocal 151

Creating a Local Variable in Python 153

Python's Global and Local Variable 154

Python's Nonlocal Variables 156

Global Keyword in Python 157

Creating Global Variables across Python Modules 160

Python Modules 161

Module Import 162

Import Statement in Python 163

Importing All Names 165

Module Search Path in Python 165

Reloading a Module 166

Dir() built-in Python function 167

Python Package 167

Number Conversion 169

Type Conversion 170

Mathematics in Python 173

Random Function in Python 174

Lists in Python 175

Nested Lists 176

Accessing Elements from a List 176

Chapter 7. Modules 179

How to Create a Module? 179

Import Statement 180

Locate a Module 186

Syntax of PYTHONPATH 187

Chapter 8. Working with Files 188

Reading from a File 191

File Pointer 192

File Access Modes 196

Writing to a File 199

Practice Exercise 200

Summary 201

Chapter 9. Object-Oriented Programming 203

Classes and Objects 204

Chapter 10. Real-World Examples of Python 217

Data Science 218

Machine Learning 219

Applications in Web Development 220

Automation 220

Things We Can Do in Python 222

Comment 223

Reading and Writing 224

Files 225

Integers 225

Triple Quotes 226

Variables 227

The Scope of a Variable 229

Modifying Values 230

The Assignment Operator 231

Chapter 11. Getting Started; Python Tips and Tricks 233

Web Scraping 233

Chapter 12. Common Programming Challenges 244

Debugging 245

Working Smart 247

User Experience 249

Estimates 251

Constant Updates 252

Problems Communicating 254

Security Concerns 255

Relying on Foreign Code 258

Lack of Planning 260

Finally 261

Conclusion 262

Introduction

There are a lot of reasons why you will love working with Python code.

It is easy to use, easy to learn, has a lot of great frameworks and libraries to work with (and we will discuss at least a few of these as we go through this guidebook), and is still powerful enough to make machine learning easy for you.

While it is possible to work with other coding languages to help you get the results you want, most people prefer to work with Python due to all of the benefits discussed.

Before we take a look at how to set up the Python environment so you can use it properly, let's take a look at a few of the different parts that come with the Python language, so you understand how a few of these codes can work for you.

The Parts You Should Know about the Python Code

First, we need to take a look at these important keywords in the Python language.

Like with what you will find in other coding languages, there is a list of keywords in Python that are meant to tell your text editor what to do.

These keywords are reserved, and you should only use them for their intended purposes if you want to be able to avoid issues with your code writing.

They are basically the commands that will tell your compiler how to behave, and they remain reserved so that you can execute the code without a lot of issues in the process.

Variables are important because they will save up spots on your computer's memory in order to hold onto parts of your code.

When you go through the process of creating a new variable, you are making sure that you are reserving some space on your computer for this.

In some cases, such as when you are working with data types, your interpreter will do the work of deciding where this information should be stored because that speeds up the process.

When it comes to working with variables, your job will be to make sure that the right variables are lining up with the right values.

This will ensure that the right parts show up in your code at the right time.

The good news is that you can give the variable the value that you want, but do check that it actually works inside of your code.

When you are ready to assign a new value to a variable, you can use the equal sign to make this happen.

Let's look at a good example of how this would work:

```
#!/usr/bin/python

counter = 10          # Assigning an integer

kilometers  = 100.0   # Assigning a floating-point

fname  = "Jordan"     # Assigning string

print counter

print kilometers

print fname
```

With the above example, you will get the results to show up with the variable that you placed with the value.

So, when the counter shows up, it will show you a 100 for the counter, 1000 for the miles, and John as the result of the name.

Next are the Python comments.

These are helpful to leave a little note in your code and can make a difference in how others are able to look through the code and know which parts are supposed to work with.

Working with the comments can be relatively easy when you are on Python.

You simply need to add the # sign in front of any comments you would like to write.

The compiler will know how to avoid that part of the code and will skip over it, without any interruption in the program.

One thing to note is how many comments you write.

While you can technically write out as many of these as you would like or that you think the code needs, try only to keep the absolutely necessary ones.

You do not want to write in so many comments that it is hard to read the rest of the code.

Just write in comments when they are needed, not all of the time.

Python statements are a simple part of the code that can make a big difference, so we are going to take some time to explore them real quick here.

Statements are going to be the part that the compiler is going to execute for you.

You can write out any kind of statement that you want, but make sure they are in the right place and that you are not using any of the keywords with them, or the compiler will get confused.

The next thing that you need to take a look at here is the functions. Functions can be another part of your language that you need to learn about. This is basically a part of the code that can be reused, and it can help to finish off one of your actions in the code.

Basically, these functions are often really effective at writing out your code without having a lot of wasted space in the code. There are a lot of functions that you can use in Python, and this can be a great benefit to the programmer.

These are just a few of the basics that come with the Python code.

We will take a closer look at doing these a bit more as we move through this guidebook, but these will help you get the Python language basics and how you can use it to your advantage in machine learning.

Getting That Environment Set Up

Now that we have had a chance to look at machine learning, some of the ways that you can benefit from and benefit from machine learning, and some of the different types of machine learning that you are able to work with, it is time to introduce some Python into this.

Python is a great coding language that you can work with, no matter what your skill level is when coding.

When it is combined with some of the ideas that come with machine learning, you will be able to see even better results in the long run.

That is why we are going to spend some time looking at how you can set up your own environment when working with the Python code.

This will help you make sure that Python is set up on your computer properly and will make it easier to work with some of the codes that we will talk about later on.

You will find along the way that the Python code is going to be a really easy one to learn compared to some of the others that are out there, and it is often one that is recommended for beginners to learn because it is simple.

But this isn't meant to fool you!

Just because you see that it is simple to work with doesn't mean that you won't be able to find the strength and the power that you need with this one.

There are a lot of different parts that you can learn about the code, but first, we are going to make sure that the environment for Python is set up in the right way to help with the Python environment with the help of machine learning.

So, to help us get this done, we need to go to the Python official website and download the Python program that we want to work with.

Then make sure that with the files you are working with, you will need to make sure the right IDE is present.

This is going to be the environment that has to be there and will ensure that you are able to write out the codes that you want to work with.

The IDE is also going to include all of the installation of Python, the debugging tools you need, and the editors.

For this specific section of machine learning, we are going to focus on the IDE for Anaconda.

This is an easy IDE to install, and it is going to have some of the development tools that you need.

It will also come with its own command-line utility, which will be so great for you installing any of the third-party software you need with it.

When you work with this IDE, you won't have to worry about doing a separate installation with the Python environment on its own.

Now we are on to the part of downloading this IDE.

There are going to be some steps that you will need to complete to make this happen.

We are going to keep these steps as simple as possible, and we are going to look at what we need to do to install this Anaconda IDE for a Windows computer.

But you will find that the steps that come with installing this on a Mac computer or a Linux computer are going to be similar to this as well.

Some of the steps that you need to use in order to help you download this kind of IDE to your computer include:

1. To start, download your preferred newest version of Python.

2. Once the executable file is downloaded, you can go over to its download folder and run the executable.

When you run this file, you should see the installation wizard come up.

Click on the "next" button.

3. Then the License Agreement dialogue box is going to appear.

   Take a minute to read this before clicking the "I Agree" button.

4. From your "Select Installation Type" box, check the "Just Me" radio button and then "next."

5. You will want to choose which installation directory you want to use before moving on.

   You should make sure that you have about 3 GB of free space on the installation directory.

6. Now you will be at the "Advanced Installation Options" dialogue box."

   You will want to select the "Register Anaconda as my default Python 3.6" and then click on "Install."

7. And then, your program will go through a few more steps, and the IDE will be installed on your program.

As you can see with all of this, setting up the Python environment that you would like to work with is going to be simple.

You just need to go through these steps to get the Anaconda IDE set up properly, and then you are able to use it for all of the codes that we will discuss in this guidebook, along with some of the other codes that you will want to write along the way.

Remember that there are some other options that you can work with when it is time to pick out an IDE that you would like to work with.

If you are doing some other work than machine learning, or you like some of the features and more that come with another IDE, you are able to download these IDEs to make it work with them as well.

But we are going to spend time working with the Anaconda IDE because it is going to have all of the features that we need to get the machine learning algorithms working the way that you would like.

Chapter 1. Basic Background of Python

Getting Started

Programming is becoming an increasingly demanded skill for anything from web design to Machine Learning and the Internet of Things.

It's on its way to having daily use due to the importance of technology.

While programming used to be a subject that people started studying for their computer science degree, now it is often taught starting from elementary school.

One of the main reasons for its widespread use is accessibility.

You don't need much to get started.

Thanks to the Internet's power, all you need is a computer and a number of software tools that you can download and install without spending a penny.

In addition, there are many resources to learn from, as well as organized communities you can join and learn from.

In this chapter, you are going to learn why Python is one of the best programming languages to start with, as well as progress your career if this isn't your first language.

Furthermore, you will explore the tools you need, install them, and start your journey.

This chapter will guide you step by step and show you everything you need to know in order to get started.

If you are already familiar with any other programming language such as C, C++, or Java, you might want to skip this chapter or simply glance through it to refresh your memory.

We can define programming as the process of designing, coding, debugging, and maintaining the source code of a computer program, which means that we say the steps to follow for the creation of the source code of computer programs.

The programming language is all the rules or regulations, symbols, and particular words used for the creation of a program, and with it, offer a solution to a particular problem.

The best-known programming languages are Basic (1964), C++ (1983), Python (1991), Java (1995), C# (2000), among others.

Programming is one of the stages for software development; programming specifies the structure and behavior of a program, verifying if it is working properly or not.

Programming includes the algorithm's specification defined as the sequence of steps and operations that the program must perform to solve a problem; for the algorithm to work, the program must be implemented in a compatible and correct language.

We could consider programming even easier than learning a new language because the programming language will be governed by a set of rules, which are, generally, always similar, so you could say that it might be considered a natural language.

In order to better understand the subject of programming, we could start with the beginnings of programming and how all this universe of languages and programs we know today began.

We could start by saying that programming began when the first computer was created in the fifteenth century when a machine capable of doing basic operations and square roots appeared (Gottfried Wilhelm von Leibniz). However, the one that actually served as a great influence for the creation of the first computer was the differential machine for calculating polynomials with the support of Lady Ada Countess (1815-1852), known as the first person who entered programming and from whom comes the name of the programming language ADA, created by the DoD (Department of the United States), in the 1970s.

Initially, it was programmed in binary codes (bi=2), in other words, it consists of strings of 0s and 1s, which is the language directly understood by the computer, or what is known as machine language, a language considered fundamental for the commuter to be thus capable of interpreting the information supplied.

Later the languages of high level appeared, using English words to give orders to follow, using intermediate processes between the language and the computer, this process can be a compiler or an interpreter.

The syntax of these programming languages is much simpler than our languages, and they use a much smaller vocabulary and set of rules.

In summary, we could say that programming is a set of sentences written in a programming language that tells the computer what tasks to perform and in what order through a series of instructions that fully detail the process.

In the world of programming languages, we find interpreted languages, such as javascript, where a program called interpreter executes the sentences while reading the text file where they are written, which is why these programs are often also called scripts.

On the other hand, we have compiled languages such as Java. In this case, we must previously convert the text file to a "translation" through a program called 'compiler' and the resulting file is the one that will finally run on the computer.

In this book, we will speak specifically of the Python programming language, being this an interpreted language whose main and most important characteristic is the application of a syntax that favors the application of readable code.

We could say that the interpreter is a type of program that executes code directly, that is to say, it does not need to be compiled, and that is the case of our target language.

What Is Python?

Python is one of the most important programming languages nowadays, being a general-purpose language.

In this book, you will have the language base so that you can start with it.

With this language, you can create a huge and varied number of applications because it allows you to create different applications since it doesn't have a defined purpose.

Why Python?

Python is a versatile and powerful programming language that was developed in 1991 by Guido van Rossum.

As a fun fact, you should know that the name of the language doesn't come from the snake, which bears the same name.

Guido named his project "Python" after Monty Python, which was a British comedy group he was a big fan of.

If you happen to be a fan as well, you will find several "Easter Eggs" within the official documentation of the language.

Since 1991, Python has been used to introduce people to programming due to its simple syntax, as well as to create complex programs or analyze massive amounts of data.

As a beginner with Python, you will be able to write a basic program quickly.

However, you can easily scale it further and turn it into a commercial project.

The main reason why Python is so popular for beginners is the fact that the language is easy to read and write.

Its structure is human-like and easy to understand; therefore, the code is very user-friendly.

This means that you shouldn't find it too difficult to remember the language and structure.

In addition, Python comes with a number of libraries and premade functions that you can immediately add to your code.

This way, you can save time.

In many ways, it's like playing with Legos.

As long as you pace yourself, learn and practice everything in this book, and extend your knowledge using other resources, you will be able to write a program that you will understand ten years from now.

Program maintenance is a crucial part of your responsibilities as a programmer, but luckily Python code is easy to administrate compared to other languages.

With that in mind, let's briefly explore the plethora of reasons why you should learn Python instead of any other languages.

After all, Python isn't quite the only language that offers you the advantages you've learned about so far.

- User-friendly: the purpose of a programming language is to form the connection between humans and computers.

    Python, like C# and Java, is a high-level programming language, which means that it is quite far from the machine language which the computer then processes.

The opposite of this is the low-level language, which usually refers to assembly language or machine code.

In other words, Python is close to English.

This allows you to write code as fast as you write any sentence, once you learn the rules and the syntax.

- Powerful: sometimes, Python is looked down upon because it is so easy to learn and it's usually the first language programmers explore, whether on their own or at computer science 101.

However, Python is a very powerful language that is just as versatile and efficient as more complex languages such as C++.

Python is used in every technical department in companies like Google, Microsoft, IBM, Xerox, NASA, and many more.

You can even use Python in game development if you prefer to practice a programming language in a more artistic way.

- OOP: Object-oriented programming is many times the optimal computer problem solver.

  It is a methodology that offers a method of defining data and actions as objects.

  This type of programming is not always necessary; however, it is usually the most optimal approach when working on large applications.

  For instance, programming languages such as C# and Java are object-oriented.

  Python can be considered an object-oriented language as well, but this feature is optional.

  The other languages don't offer such versatility.

  This means that with Python, you don't necessarily have to learn the object-oriented methodology from the start.

  This is one of the reasons why it's so much easier to start programming with Python than C++.

  However, you have the massive benefits of OOP at your fingertips, but only when you actually need it.

  If you are working on a basic program, there's no need for it.

Python offers you all the power and versatility you need.

- Computer-friendly: you can run Python on any kind of computer.

You don't need a powerful computer processing unit and a great deal of RAM to start programming.

You can even use a credit-card-sized computer like the Raspberry Pi.

In fact, Python requires so little that it is one of the top languages used in creating little robots that are operated by $5 computers.

In addition, Python runs on any operating system, whether it's Linux, Windows, or Mac.

The programs you write do not depend on the platform.

You can work on an application on your Windows running computer and then switch it to your Mac.

For instance, if you finished creating a program and you need beta testers, you can email your project to a friend that uses Linux and another one with Windows. The program will work.

- Language adaptability: if you ever write a program in another language, you can integrate Python within it.

   In other words, you can use Python on a program that was written in Java.

   In addition, you also combine Python with another language in order to take advantage of the benefits that are offered by both of them.

   For instance, you can integrate C or C++ in order to benefit from the system optimization and speed that they offer.

- It's free: everyone likes free stuff, and Python won't cost you a cent.

   You can always download and install it for free as many times as you want.

   In addition, Python is an open-source language, which means that the license even allows you to make modifications to the source code.

   This means that you can modify Python and then sell your own version of it.

You might not be interested in these features at this point, but it is one of the reasons why it's such a popular language.

- Community: being a powerful and versatile open source programming language brings benefit to the community.

There are many online communities dedicated to teaching and learning everything there is to know about Python.

You can ask questions on online boards or seek the advice of a master programmer.

You can also seek fellow students and work on a project together.

Python's popularity has gathered a massive crowd around it, and you should take advantage of it.

Installing Python

Before you can start programming, you need to download and install Python on your machine.

The installation is quite straightforward no matter what operating system you're running; however, you do need to pay attention to a couple of things.

First, you need to head to Python's homepage and head to the "Downloads" section.

There you will see a number of different installers, and each one of them has a different version.

Make sure to download the right installer that matches your computer's operating system and select the latest version.

Once the download is complete, run the installer and follow the steps.

You should simply accept the standard settings, and once the installation is complete, you're ready to go.

If you don't want to install Python for some reason, you may notice that you have some kind of a console on the website's homepage.

This is a Python online console, and you can use it to practice your coding skills or to try out some of the examples in this book.

It's advisable for you to type the code yourself, even if you copy it from the book, and then try to be creative with it.

You need to practice in order to memorize the syntax and specific commands, and the online console is really handy for a quick practice session. Using a Text Editor

Python programming can be done with nearly any kind of plain text editor.

You can use programs like Notepad, Notepad++, gedit, and many more.

Keep in mind that some of these text editors come with a variety of features that are useful to programmers.

For instance, some of them, such as Notepad++ offer syntax highlighting which will instantly show you any errors you made.

If you type code in a basic editor like plain Notepad, the program won't tell you when you've forgotten a semicolon or if you added additional space.

There are many programs to choose from, so pick any editor you feel comfortable with.

With that in mind, avoid using word processors such as Microsoft Word or Open Office.

They aren't good for programming purposes.

They can be used to write code; however, the problem is that when saving it, the program will sneak in some additional lines of code by itself.

That code is specific to the word processor, and it can impact your program's speed, or even worse, it will simply not run.

Using an IDE

An IDE, which stands for Integrated Development Environment, is a program designed with a number of features that are useful to programmers.

It has a graphical interface, and it makes typing code much faster due to autocomplete and history functions.

Programming stays the same whether you are using a text editor or an IDE. However, with the IDE, you will benefit from many shortcuts, reminders, error signaling, and code autocorrect.

Many IDE's even include suggestions on how to fix an error.

There are many IDE's to choose from, but one of the most popular ones is IDLE.

It comes in the same package as Python, so there's no need to perform any extra steps.

Keep in mind that it can run in two modes, namely interactive and script.

Use interactive if you want Python to respond to whatever commands you type immediately.

Your First Program

Now that your toolkit is prepared, it's time to write your first program.

For this example, we'll use IDLE because it's important to get used to IDE's from the start in order to avoid any future frustrations.

If you prefer to use a text editor or the online Python console, go ahead, the code will work the same.

Now, start running IDLE in interactive mode.

You will now see a window that is known as a Python shell.

At the command prompt, type the following line:

print ("Hello World!")

Now you should see the result displayed on your screen like the following: Hello World!

That's it!

Congratulations, you can call yourself a programmer now.

Now let's discuss this bit of code briefly.

The first thing you'll notice is that Python code is plain English, easy to read and understand.

Even without programming knowledge, you probably knew what this line of code would do because it's self-explanatory.

That's the beauty of working with Python.

As for the command we used, "print ()" is a function that displays the text which is written in the parentheses.

Keep in mind that the line needs to be surrounded by quotation marks; otherwise, you'll get an error.

Furthermore, pay attention to how you type the function because, in Python, everything is case sensitive.

The command "print" will work. However, if you type it as "Print," it will not.

Now, let's create the same program but this time by using IDLE's script mode.

Don't forget that interactive mode gives you instant results.

It works the same as the online Python shell.

However, you won't be able to save your program so that you can continue working on it later.

In order to save it and edit it later, you need to work in script mode.

You can run IDLE in script mode simply by clicking on "File" and selecting "New Window."

Now type the same line again:

print ("Hello World!)

Hit the Enter key.

You'll notice that nothing happens.

That's because you are writing a list of instructions that will be executed at a later date when you run the program.

First, you need to save the application by clicking on "Save As". from the "File" menu.

You'll notice that by default, the file has the "py" extension.

Always make sure your scripts are saved this way in order to be recognized as Python programs.

Now, if you run the program, IDLE will open the interactive mode window and display the result.

For now, you've run your "Hello World" program by using IDLE.

However, you normally want your applications to run like the ones you are currently using.

This means you want an executable file that you double click and it runs.

At the moment, if you click on the Python file, a window will open and then close abruptly.

You may be thinking that the program doesn't work because nothing happened; however, something did happen.

It was simply too fast for you to observe anything concrete.

The program executed all of its instructions, which means that it displayed the message in a fraction of a second, and then it terminated itself.

What you need to do is keep the program running once it executes all of its commands so that you can see the results and interact with them.

But before you do that, let's take a moment to discuss how to comment on your code and make it readable and easy to understand.

Code Comments and Your Program

Open your script and type the following lines:

\# Hello World!

\# This is a demonstration of the "print" function.

If you run the program again, you will see that nothing changed.

These lines you added aren't executed as code.

They are known as comments, and their purpose is to make the code of an application more understandable.

You might be thinking that typing such information is a waste of time because, as the programmer, you already know what your code is about.

That may be true; however, when you write a complex program, and then you abandon it for a week or two, you're going to have some trouble understanding the purpose of every function and variable.

Sure, you can read your code and eventually figure everything out, but that is not the proper use of your time.

Code comments are used to label and explain complicated functions so that you don't have to dive into the code itself.

They are especially useful if another programmer is going to work on your program at a later date.

Imagine a stranger having to decipher your personal approach to the development of your application.

On a large project, he could waste wakes of his time instead of doing some work in order to progress.

Comments are defined by the hash mark in front of a line.

Each line you intend as a comment needs to have its own mark; otherwise, you will get an error.

If you're worried about your programs' efficiency due to hundreds or even thousands of comments, you shouldn't be.

They have no impact on your computer because when the code is executed, the machine ignores all comments and uses no additional resources.

Additionally, to make your comments and code more readable, you can leave empty lines.

However, don't do this after every line of code.

Use an empty space in between blocks of code or sections.

Programs ignore blank space, so nothing will be affected by using it.

Now let's get back to your first program.

Add the following line after the print function:

input ("\n\n Hit the Enter key to exit!")

This line will display the console in which the line "Hello World!" is printed and then display the line "Hit the Enter key to exit!"

Finally, the program will stay open and wait for you until you hit the Enter key.

This is a simple way to keep the program running until the user performs an action.

Chapter 2. Data Types in Python

Every program has certain data that allows it to function and operate in the way we want.

The data can be a text, a number, or any other thing in between.

Whether complex or as simple as you like, these data types are the cogs in a machine that allow the rest of the mechanism to connect and work.

Python is a host to a few data types, and, unlike its competitors, it does not deal with an extensive range of things.

That is good because we have less to worry about and yet achieve accurate results despite the lapse.

Python was created to make our lives, as programmers, a lot easier.

Strings

In Python and other programming languages, any text value that we may use, such as names, places, sentences, are all referred to as strings.

A string is a collection of characters, not words or letters, which is marked by the use of single or double quotation marks.

To display a string, use the print command, open up a parenthesis, put in a quotation mark, and write anything.

Once done, we generally end the quotation marks and close the bracket.

Since we are using PyCharm, the IntelliSense detects what we are about to do and delivers the rest for us immediately.

You may have noticed how it jumped to the rescue when you only type in the opening bracket.

It will automatically provide you with a closing one.

Similarly, for the quotation marks, one or two, it will provide the closing ones for you.

See why we are using PyCharm?

It greatly helps us out.

"I do have a question. Why do we use either single or double quotation marks if both provide the same result?"

Ah! Quite the eye.

There is a reason we use these, let me explain by using the example below:

print('I'm afraid I won't be able to make it')

print("He said 'Why do you care?'")

Try and run this through PyCharm.

Remember, to run, simply click on the green play-like button on the top right side of the interface.

"C:\Users\Programmer\AppData\Local\Programs\Python\Python37-32\python.exe" "C:/Users/Programmer/PycharmProjects/PFB/Test1.py"

  File "C:/Users/Programmer/PycharmProjects/PFB/Test1.py", line 1

print('I'm afraid I won't be able to make it')

      ^

SyntaxError: invalid syntax

Process finished with exit code 1

Here's a hint: That's an error!

So what happened here?

Try and revisit the inputs.

See how we started the first print statement with a single quote?

Immediately, we ended the quote using another quotation mark.

The program only accepted the letter 'I' as a string.

You may have noticed how the color may have changed for every other character from 'm' until 'won,' after which the program detects yet another quotation mark and accepts the rest as another string.

Quite confusing, to be honest.

Similarly, in the second statement, the same thing happened.

The program saw double quotes and understood it as a string, right until the point the second instance of double quotation marks arrives.

That's where it did not bother checking whether it is a sentence or that it may have still been going on. Computers do not understand English; they understand binary communications.

The compiler is what runs when we press the run button.

It compiles our code and interprets the same into a series of ones and zeros so that the computer may understand what we are asking it to do.

This is exactly why the second it spots the first quotation mark, it considers it as a start of a string and ends it immediately when it spots a second quotation mark, even if the sentence was carrying onwards.

To overcome this obstacle, we use a mixture of single and double quotes when we know we need to use one of these within the sentence.

Try and replace the opening and closing quotation marks in the first state as double quotation marks on both ends.

Likewise, change the quotation marks for the second statement to single quotation marks as shown here:

print("I'm afraid I won't be able to make it")

print('He said "Why do you care?"')

Now the output should look like this:

I'm afraid I won't be able to make it

He said, "Why do you care?"

Lastly, for strings, the naming convention does not apply to the text of the string itself.

You can use regular English writing methods and conventions without worries, as long as that is within the quotation marks.

Anything outside it will not be a string in the first place and will or may not work if you change the cases.

Did you know that strings also use triple quotes?

Never heard that before, have you?

We will cover that shortly!

Numeric Data Type

Just as the number suggests, Python is able to recognize numbers rather well.

The numbers are divided into two pairs:

- **Integer** – A positive and/or negative whole numbers that are represented without any decimal points.

- **Float** – A real number that has a decimal point representation.

This means, if you were to use 100 and 100.00, one would be identified as an integer while the other will be deemed as a float.

So why do we need to use two various number representations?

If you are designing a program, suppose a small game that has a character's life of 10, you might wish to keep the program in a way that whenever a said character takes a hit, his life reduces by one or two points.

However, to make things a little more precise, you may need to use float numbers.

Now, each hit might vary and may take 1.5, 2.1, or 1.8 points away from the life total.

Using floats allows us to use greater precision, especially when calculations are on the cards.

If you aren't too troubled about the accuracy, or your programming involves whole numbers only, stick to integers.

Booleans

Ah! The one with the funny name.

Boolean (or bool) is a data type that can only operate on and return two values: True or False.

Booleans are a vital part of any program, except the ones where you may never need them, such as our first program.

These are what allow programs to take various paths if the result is true or false.

Here's a little example.

Suppose you are traveling to a country you have never been to.

There are two choices you are most likely to face.

If it is cold, you will be packing your winter clothes.

If it is warm, you will be packing clothes that are appropriate for warm weather.

Simple, right?

That is exactly how the Booleans work.

We will look into the coding aspect of it as well.

For now, just remember, when it comes to true and false, you are dealing with a bool value.

List

While this is slightly more advanced for someone at this stage of learning, the list is a data type that does what it sounds like.

It lists objects, values, or stores data within square brackets ([]).

Here's what a list would look like:

month = ['Jan', 'Feb', 'March', 'And so on!']

We will be looking into this separately, where we will discuss lists, tuples, and dictionaries.

We have briefly discussed these data types.

Surely, they are used within Python, but how?

If you think you can type in the numbers and true and false, all on their own, it will never work.

Variables

You have the passengers, but you do not have a mode of commuting; they will have nowhere to go.

These passengers would just be folks standing around, waiting for some kind of transportation to pick them up.

Similarly, data types cannot function alone.

They need to be 'stored' in these vehicles, which can take them places.

As we programmers refer to as containers, these special vehicles are called 'variables,' and they are the elements that perform the magic for us.

Variables are specialized containers that store a specific value in them and can then be accessed, called, modified, or even removed when the need arises.

Every variable that you may create will hold a specific type of data in them.

You cannot add more than one type of data within a variable.

In other programming languages, you will find that in order to create a variable, you need to use the keyword 'var' followed by an equals mark '=' and then the value.

In Python, it is a lot easier, as shown below:

name = "John"

age = 33

weight = 131.50

is_married = True

In the above, we have created a variable named 'name' and given it a value of characters.

If you recall strings, we have used double quotation marks to let the program know that this is a string.

We then created a variable called age.

Here, we simply wrote 33, which is an integer, as there are no decimal figures following that.

You do not need to use quotation marks here at all.

Next, we created a variable 'weight' and assigned it a float value.

Finally, we created a variable called 'is_married' and assigned it a 'True' bool value.

If you were to change the 'T' to 't,' the system will not recognize it as a bool and will end up giving an error.

Focus on how we used the naming convention for the last variable.

We will be ensuring that our variables follow the same naming convention.

You can even create blank variables if you feel like you may need these at a later point in time or wish to initiate them at no value at the start of the application.

For variables with numeric values, you can create a variable with a name of your choosing and assign it a value of zero.

Alternatively, you can create an empty string as well by using opening and closing quotation marks only.

empty_variable1 = 0

empty_variable2 = ""

You do not have to name them like this necessarily, you can come up with more meaningful names so that you and any other programmer who may read your code would understand.

I have given them these names to ensure anyone can immediately understand their purpose.

Now we have learned how to create variables, let's learn how to call them.

What's the point of having these variables if we are never going to use them, right?

Let's create a new set of variables.

Have a look here:

name = "James"

age = 43

height_in_cm = 163

occupation = "Programmer"

I do encourage you to use your own values and play around with variables if you like.

In order for us to call the name variable, we simply need to type the name of the variable.

To print that to the console, we will do this:

print(name)

Output

James

The same goes for age, the height variable, and occupation.

But what if we wanted to print them together and not separately?

Try running the code below and see what happens:

print(name age height_in_cm occupation)

Surprised? Did you end up with this?

print(name age height_in_cm occupation)
              ^

SyntaxError: invalid syntax

Process finished with exit code 1

Here is the reason why that happened.

When you were using a single variable, the program knew what variable that was.

The minute you added a second, a third, and a fourth variable, it tried to look for something that was written in that manner.

Since there wasn't any, it returned with an error that otherwise says:

"Umm... Are you sure, Sir? I tried looking everywhere, but I couldn't find this 'name age height_in_cm occupation' element anywhere."

All you need to do is add a comma to act as a separator like so:

print(name, age, height_in_cm, occupation)

Output:

James 43 163 Programmer

"Your variables, Sir!"

And now, it knew what we were talking about.

The system recalled these variables and was successfully able to show us what their values were.

But what happens if you try to add two strings together?

What if you wish to merge two separate strings and create a third-string as a result?

first_name = "John"

last_name = "Wick"

To join these two strings into one, we can use the '+' sign.

The resulting string will now be called a String Object, and since this is Python we are dealing with, everything within this language is considered as an object, thus the Object-Oriented Programming nature that we discussed somewhere in the start.

first_name = "John"

last_name = "Wick"

first_name + last_name

Here, we did not ask the program to print the two strings.

If you wish to print these two instead, simply add the print function and type in the string variables with a + sign in the middle within parentheses.

Sounds good, but the result will not be quite what you expect:

first_name = "John"

last_name = "Wick"

print(first_name + last_name)

Output:

JohnWick

Hmm. Why do you think that happened?

Certainly, we did use a space between the two variables.

The problem is that the two strings have combined together, quite literally here, and we did not provide a white space (blank space) after John or before Wick; it will not include that.

Even the white space can be a part of a string.

To test it out, add one character of space within the first line of code by tapping on the friendly spacebar after John.

Now try running the same command again and you should see "John Wick" as your result.

The process of merging two strings is called concatenation.

While you can concatenate as many strings as you like, you cannot concatenate a string and an integer together.

If you really need to do that, you will need to use another technique to convert the integer into a string first and then concatenate the same.

To convert an integer, we use the *str()* function.

text1 = "Zero is equal to "

text2 = 0

print(text1 + str(text2))

Output:

Zero is equal to 0

Python reads the codes in a line-by-line method.

First, it will read the first line, then the second, then third, and so on.

This means we can do a few things beforehand as well, to save some time for ourselves.

text1 = "Zero is still equal to"

text2 = str(0)

print(text1 + text2)

Output:

Zero is still equal to 0

You may wish to remember this as we will be visiting the conversion of values into strings a lot sooner than you might expect.

There is one more way through which you can print out both string variables and numeric variables, all at the same time, without the need for '+' signs or conversion.

This way is called String Formatting.

To create a formatted string, we follow a simple process as shown here:

print(f" This is where {var 1} will be. Then {var 2}, then {var 3} and so on")

Var 1, 2, and 3 are variables.

You can have as many as you like here.

Notice the importance of whitespace.

Try not to use the spacebar as much.

You might struggle at the start but will eventually get the hang of it.

When we start the string, we place the character 'f' to let Python know that this is a formatted string.

Here, the curly brackets are performing a part of placeholders.

Within these curly brackets, you can recall your variables.

One set of curly brackets will be a placeholder for each variable that you would like to call upon.

To put this in practical terms, let's look at an example:

show = "GOT"

name1 = "Daenerys"

name2 = "Jon"

name3 = "Tyrion"

seasons = 8

print(f "The show called {show} had characters like {name1}, {name2} and {name3} in all {seasons} seasons. ")

Output:

The show called GOT had characters like Daenerys, Jon, and Tyrion in all 8 seasons.

While there are other variations to convert integers into strings and concatenate strings together, it is best to learn those, which are used throughout the industry as standard.

Remember the triple quotes mentioned earlier?

I believe you are in a good position now to begin using those.

Have a look at this result, and keep in mind that I did not use any variable here at all.

Now, you have seen how to create a variable, recall it, and concatenate the same.

Everything sounds perfect, except for one thing; These are predefined values.

What if we need an input directly from the end-user?

How can we possibly know that?

Even if we do, where do we store them?

User-Input Values

Suppose we are trying to create an online form.

This form will contain simple questions like asking for the user's name, age, city, email address, and so on.

There must be some way through which we can allow users to input these values on his/her own and for us to get those back.

We can use the same to print out a message that thanks the users for using the form and that they will be contacted at their email address for further steps.

To do that, we will use the *input()* function.

The input function can accept any kind of input.

In order to use this function, we will need to provide it with some reference so that the end-user is able to know what he/she is about to fill out.

Let us look at a typical example and see how such a form can be created:

print("Hello and welcome to my interactive tutorial.")

name = input("Your Name: ")

age = int(input("Your age: "))

city = input("Where do you live? ")

email = input("Please enter your email address: ")

print(f"Thank you very much {name}, you will be contacted at {email}.")

Output:

Hello and welcome to my interactive tutorial.

Your Name: **Sam**

Your age: **28**

Where do you live? **London**

Please enter your email address: ***sam@something.com***

Thank you very much Sam, you will be contacted at sam@something.com.

In the above, we began by printing a greeting to the user and welcoming them to the tutorial.

Next, we created a variable named 'name' and assigned it a value that our user will generously provide us with.

In the age, you may have noticed I changed the input to *int()*, just as we changed integer to string earlier on.

This is because our message within the input parameters is a string value by default, as it is within quotation marks.

You will always need to ensure you know what type of value you are after and do the needful, as shown above.

Next, we asked for the name of the city and the email address.

Now, using a formatted string, we printed out our final message.

"Wait! How can we print out something we have yet to receive or know?"

I did mention that Python works line by line.

The program will start with a greeting, as shown in the output.

It will then move to the next line and realize that it must wait for the user to input something and hit enter.

This is why the input value has been highlighted by bold and italic fonts here.

The program then moves to the next line and waits yet again for the user to put something in and press enter, and this goes on until the final input command is sorted.

Now the program has the values stored; it immediately recalls these values and prints them out for the viewer to see in the end.

The result was rather pleasing as it gave a personalized message to the user, and we received the information we need.

Everybody walks away, happy!

Storing information directly from the user is both essential and, at times, necessary.

Imagine a game that is based on Python.

The game is rather simple, where a ball will jump when you tap the screen.

The problem is, your screen isn't responding to the touch at all for some reason.

While that happens, the program will either keep the ball running until an input is detected, or it will just not work at all.

We also use input functions to gather information such as login ID and passwords to match with the database, but that is a point that we shall discuss later when we will talk about statements.

It is a little more complicated than it sounds now, but once you understand how to use statements, you will be one step closer than ever before becoming a programmer.

Chapter 3. Operators - The Types and Their Uses

Operators are pretty much how they sound like.

They operate as per our needs and connect two dots together.

That was the simplest way I can explain these.

However, there are quite a few operators available when it comes to Python.

They are used for various purposes and are seemingly being used in every program that will be created, apart from the ones where you are only relying on print statements.

I shall not waste a lot of time here, so let us get straight to business and see the types first and then move a little towards their uses, both including quite a bit of arithmetic as well.

Not a fan of arithmetic myself, but then again, it is necessary!

The Types

Straight away, we begin by seeing some basic ones.

When we talk about arithmetic, the first few things to pop-up are the addition, subtraction, multiplication, and division signs. Python is no stranger to these, either.

There are a lot of applications and programs designed using these. We will be looking into those too, I promise.

+, -, /, *

The above signs, not including the comma marks, are universal in nature.

Whether you speak English, Japanese, or Mandarin, you know you are dealing with some basic operators.

These operators are in use throughout the world, at least within a calculator.

Hopefully, using these within Python at this point in time should not be a problem for you.

However, these are not the only operators we use.

The '=' sign, if you may recall, is not an 'equal to' sign in Python.

It is an operator that assigns a value to a variable.

To equate something, we use the '==' sign.

I am sure you had already figured that out.

What about these, then?

!=

>=

<=

%

//

**

+=

Saving the last one, which is technically called an augmented assignment operator, the remainder might seem a little different.

Don't worry, I am here to explain these.

!=

This is the "Not equal to" operator.

You will normally find this in use within statements to compare scenarios and create conditions that are not equal to something.

How does that work?

Here's a simple version.

We will look into a more complex one after this.

x = 28

y = 19

print(x != y)

Output:

True

The output value here will not be a number, but a Boolean value of 'True.'

Here's a more complex-natured one. Suppose you have a list of questions for the user to check for loan approval.

One of these questions will have "Do you have any criminal convictions or recorded history?" to which the banks will automatically refuse.

In a programming language, we will create an 'if' statement and use the same details as under:

age = 28

is_working = True

is_married = False

has_criminal_record = False

if has_criminal_record != True:

print("You are eligible for a loan!")

else:

print("Sorry, but you are ineligible for a loan")

Assuming that we fill these out, the application will automatically print out that the person is eligible for a loan.

However, change has_criminal_record to True and then run the program.

Now the program will execute the 'else' statement as has_criminal_record now matches 'True' and, therefore, renders the 'if' condition void.

>= and <=

The "greater and equal to" and the "lesser and equal to" operators were already used by us at least once.

These are used in a similar fashion to the '!=' operator.

However, owing to these operators' nature, we use these for numbers, either integers or floats.

These are also called comparison operators, and so is '!=' and '==' operators.

Let us put these to some use and see how they function.

Mind you, this one will take a little closer look.

I have designed it deliberately to intimidate you.

If you read closely, you will immediately realize how easy it is to understand what's going on here.

print("Welcome to our online eligibility checker!")

age = int(input("Enter your age: "))

has_license = input("Do you have a license? [Y/N]: ")

if has_license.lower() == "y":

has_license = True

else:

has_license = False

salary = int(input("Your monthly Salary: $"))

if age <= 35:

print("The age is right!")

```
if has_license == True:

    print("You have a valid license.")

    if salary >= 3500:

        print("Perfect! You are eligible.")

    else:

        print("I am sorry but you are below our minimum requirement")

else:

    print("Sorry, but you need to have a valid license")

else:

print("You are above our maximum age limit.")
```

I have created a little eligibility checker here to see whether a person is eligible for service.

Here, you will find most of the comparative operators at work.

I have also given this code a bit of freedom.

Now, we do not have to put in the values manually any longer.

The user can put in the required values, and the program will run through instantly to deliver results accordingly.

Go ahead, try out the program, and see how it works for you.

Once again, I highly encourage you to change the values, modify the program, and see how it works.

The more you experiment, the quicker you will learn.

For the above, as long as all conditions are met, this will be the output:

Welcome to our online eligibility checker!

Enter your age: **28**

Do you have a license? [Y/N]: **y**

Your monthly Salary: $**4000**

The age is right!

You have a valid license.

Perfect! You are eligible.

While everything seems to be going perfectly so far, did you happen to notice something new within the code?

Look again at the first 'if' statement.

Right at the start of the condition, I used has_license.lower(), what do you think that is?

The variable I created was assigned some built-in methods, and I accessed one of those named *lower()*.

They are much like functions, but instead of having massive blocks of codes within them, they only do one purpose.

In this case, I wanted to ensure that whatever the user inputs, it gets converted to lowercase to match with the condition.

Since Python is a case-sensitive language, had I left the value as 'Y,' the condition would have never met.

To access the list of methods available, after the name of a variable, type a period '.' and the list of methods would open up.

Let us move on to the remaining three so that we can then discuss something equally important—the operator precedence.

The '%' is called the modulus operator.

This basically returns the remainder value from the equation.

Let's try this out:

alpha = 20

beta = 11

print(alpha % beta)

Output:

9

This operator first divides the two numbers and then brings forth the remainder as there is no further division possible.

You can try and change the value of alpha to 200, and the remainder will be two.

The '/' is a straightforward division operator.

Replace the modulus sign above (alpha at 20) with the division sign, and you get the following result:

1.8181818181818181

Now, the point to note here is that we entered two integers, and the return value was afloat.

What if we just wish to settle for an integer instead?

That's where we use the '//' sign.

Now, use this sign instead of the division sign.

The result should be '1' only.

The result will not be rounded off to the nearest tenth.

This is the floor division operator, which always returns an integer value.

If, however, you wish to round off the value, you will need to use a function called *round()*, and this is how you will do so:

alpha = 20

beta = 11

print(round(alpha / beta))

Output:

2

Finally, we have the '**' signs.

These are exponential operators.

Now, replace the division operator with the exponential operator, remove the round function, and you will get the following result:

204800000000000

Ah! If only we had that many digits in our accounts!

Well, now that we have seen the operators and their types, let us discuss a little about the operator precedence.

The Operator Precedence

What do you think would be the outcome of this simple calculation?

print(10 + 20 - 5 * 4 / 2 ** 2)

400? 20? No! The answer would be 25.

Why?

Because there is specific precedence that operators follow.

There are some who take higher priority and are calculated first.

Here is a simple way to explain things:

Exponentiate > Divide > Multiply > Add/Subtract

That is always the case in Python.

And with that, we can say goodbye to some basic operators and go to a little more advanced once.

The Logical Operators

To explain this a little more clearly, let us create a scenario.

You are asked to create a program that checks for someone's eligibility for a mortgage based on certain values and inputs.

You are told that there are questions like asking the name, age, and then there are two major factors that will influence the decision.

These pertain to the applicant having a good or bad credit history and having a high income of at least $5,000 per month.

To create this, we can certainly do what I did earlier on by using nested conditional statements, but at times, they may not be the best option to go for.

Instead, we use logical operators to do the hard work for us.

How?

Let's find out, shall we?

```
print("Eligibility Checker 101")

name = input("Please enter your name: ")

age = int(input("Please enter your age: "))

salary = int(input("What is your monthly salary? "))

min_salary = 5000

has_good_credit = True

if salary >= min_salary and has_good_credit:
```

print(f"Congratulations {name}, You are eligible for a mortgage.")

else:

print(f"{name}, it appears you may not be eligible at this time")

The first logical operator we have here is the 'and' operator.

What that does is create a condition where both the former and the latter must be met.

If not, the entire block of code will not be considered, and the 'else' statement will be executed instead.

Note: See how I did not assign any comparison operator for the has_good_credit?

That's because the value for that is a bool value, which is currently set to true!

If you read this code in plain English, it literally reads:

"If the salary is equal to or higher than the minimum salary and has good credit."

Now, let us type in the values to see if this works:

Eligibility Checker 101

Please enter your name: **Smith**

Please enter your age: **34**

What is your monthly salary? **5000**

Congratulations Smith, You are eligible for a mortgage.

Now, let's try to change the bool value to 'False' and see what happens:

Eligibility Checker 101

Please enter your name: **Snow**

Please enter your age: **30**

What is your monthly salary? **6000**

Snow, it appears you may not be eligible at this time

This happened because the first condition is met, but the second condition was not satisfied.

So, you submitted the program, and a few days later, the client returns and says, "Well, I would like you to change the program a little.

This time, we want our applicants to either have a good salary or good credit. Anyone would do!"

Now, let us look at the code again.

How can we do that without changing much?

That is where the second logical operator comes in.

The 'or' operator is used in such situations where one or the other condition is true, in which case the program will execute the 'if' statement block.

Let us try it out by changing the 'and' to 'or' and keeping the has_good_credit value to false.

print("Eligibility Checker 101")

name = input("Please enter your name: ")

age = int(input("Please enter your age: "))

salary = int(input("What is your monthly salary? "))

min_salary = 5000

has_good_credit = False

if salary >= min_salary or has_good_credit:

print(f"Congratulations {name}, You are eligible for a mortgage.")

else:

print(f"{name}, it appears you may not be eligible at this time")

Output:

Eligibility Checker 101

Please enter your name: Nathan

Please enter your age: 28

What is your monthly salary? 6000

Congratulations Nathan, You are eligible for a mortgage.

Now, the code was successfully executed and gave Nathan the good news.

This is because the 'or' operator informed Python, "Hey! Even if one of these conditions is applicable, go ahead!"

Lo and behold! The world of logical operators.

They make our lives so much easier, don't they?

Lastly, we also have one more logical operator called 'not operator'.

This is slightly tricky to understand but bear with me on this one.

Suppose the same client returns and asks, "Hey! Good job, but I need another change. This time, I want you to code your program so that it only works if the applicant has a good salary and not good credit."

Sure, and to do just that, this is what we will do:

print("Eligibility Checker 101")

name = input("Please enter your name: ")

age = int(input("Please enter your age: "))

salary = int(input("What is your monthly salary? "))

min_salary = 5000

has_good_credit = False

if salary >= min_salary and not has_good_credit:

print(f"Congratulations {name}, You are eligible for a mortgage.")

else:

print(f"{name}, it appears you may not be eligible at this time")

What the 'not' operator does is it changes the value of the second variable from True to False, or from False to True.

In this case, since the applicant has no credit history, the condition fits.

The interpreter will see this as "Applicant has a salary that is greater than the minimum and does not have a good credit history, which is true, then let's go with it!"

The result will be as follows:

Eligibility Checker 101

Please enter your name: Nicole

Please enter your age: 29

What is your monthly salary? 8000

Congratulations Nicole, You are eligible for a mortgage.

If you were to change the bool value to true, Nicole here would be left a little sad.

And that about wraps up our trip to the world of operators.

We saw the types, and we saw their usages as well.

These do take a little while to be understood fully but rest assured, they are super helpful.

Continue practicing these codes and use your own imagination to come up with situations and scenarios where you may be able to use these effectively.

Chapter 4. Loops and Functions

LOOPS

if...else Flow Control

The if..else statement in Python is a decision making when executing the program.

The if...else statement will ONLY execute code if the specified condition exists.

The syntax of if...else in Python

if test expression:

Statement(s)

Discussion

The python program will only execute the statements(s) if the test expression is True.

The program first evaluates the test expression before executing the statement(s).

The program will not execute the statement(s) if the test expression is False.

By convention, the body of it is marked by indentation while the first is not indented line signals the end.

Challenge: Think of scenarios, real-life, where the if...else condition is required.

- If you have not enrolled for a course, then you cannot sit for the exam; else, sit for the exam.

- If you have paid for house rent, then you will be issued with acknowledgment receipt else request for more time.

- If you are a licensed driver, then you can drive to school; else, you hire a taxi.

- If you are tired, then you can watch movies else can complete the essay.

- If you are an ethical person, then you will acknowledge your mistake; else, you will overlook the damage caused.

- If you are committed to programming, then you will practice daily; else, you will lose interest.

- If you have signed for email alerts, you will be updated frequently; else, you will have to check the website daily.

- If you plead guilty to all accounts, you are likely to be convicted; else, your case's merit will depend on cross-examination of witnesses and evidence presented.

Note: When we use the if statement alone without the else part, it will only print/display if the condition is true, it will not cater to the alternative, the case where the first condition is not present.

Example 1

Start IDLE.

Navigate to the File menu and click New Window.

Type the following:

number=5

if number>0   #The comparison operator

   print(number, "The number is a positive number")

Discussion

The program contains the if the condition that tests if the given number satisfies the if condition, "is it greater than 0" since 5 is greater than zero, the condition is satisfied the interpreter is allowed to execute the next statement which is to extract and display the numerical value including the string message.

The test condition in this program is "number>0.

But think of when the condition is not met, what happens? Let us look at Example 2.

Example 2

Start IDLE.

Navigate to the File menu and click New Window.

Type the following:

number=-9

if number>0:

  print(number, "This is a positive number")

Discussion

The program contains only the if statement, which tests the expression by testing of -9 is greater than zero since it is not the interpreter will not execute the subsequent program code lines.

In real life, you will want to provide for an alternate in case the first condition is not met.

This program will not display anything when executed because the 'if' condition has not been met.

The test condition in this program is "number>0.

Practice Exercise

Write programs in Python using if statement only to perform the following:

- Given number=7, write a program to test and display only even numbers.

- Given number1=8, number2=13, write a program to only display if the sum is less than 10.

- Given count_int=57, write a program that tests if the count is more than 45 and displays, the count is above the recommended number.

- Given marks=34, write a program that tests if the marks are less than 50 and display the message, the score is below average.

- Given marks=78, write a program that tests if the marks are more than 50 and display the message, great performance.

- Given number=88, write a program that tests if the number is an odd number and displays the message, Yes it is an odd number.

- Given number=24, write a program that tests and displays if the number is even.

- Given number =21, write a program that tests if the number is odd and displays the string, Yes it is an odd number.

Note

The execution of statements after the if expression will only happen where the if the expression evaluates to True; otherwise, the statements are ignored.

if…else statement in Python

The if…else syntax

if test condition:

   Statements

else:

   Statements

The explanation the if statement, the if…else statement will execute the body of if in the case that the test condition is True.

Should the if…else test expression evaluate to false, the body of the else will be executed.

Program blocks are denoted by indentation.

The if...else provides more maneuverability when placing conditions on the code.

Example

A program that checks whether a number is positive or negative

Start IDLE.

Navigate to the File menu and click New Window.

Type the following:

number_mine=-56

if(number<0):

   print(number_mine, "The number is negative")

else:

   print(number_mine, "The number is a positive number")

Practice Exercise

Write a Python program that uses if..else flow control to perform the following

- Given number=9, write a program that tests and displays whether the number is even or odd.

- Given marks=76, write a program that tests and displays whether the marks are above the pass mark or not, bearing in mind that the pass mark is 50.

- Given number=78, write a program that tests and displays whether the number is even or odd.

- Given marks=27, write a program that tests and displays whether the marks are above the pass mark or not, bearing in mind that the pass mark is 50.

Challenge:

Write a program that accepts age input from the user, explicitly convert the age into integer data types, then uses if…else flow control to tests whether the person is underage or not, the legal age is 21.

Include comments and indentation to improve the readability of the program.

if…elif…else Flow Control Statement in Python

Now think of scenarios where we need to evaluate multiple conditions, not just one, not just two, but three and more.

Think of where you have to choose team members, if not Richard, then Mercy, if not Richard and Mercy, then Brian, if not Richard, Mercy, and Brian, then Yvonne.

Real-life scenarios may involve several choices/conditions that have to be captured when writing a program.

if...elif..else Syntax

if test expression:

   Body of if

elif test expression:

   Body of elif

else:

   Body of else

Remember that the elif simply refers to else if and is intended to allow for checking of multiple expressions.

The if block is evaluated first, then elif block(s), before the else block.

In this case, the else block is more of a fallback option when all other conditions return false.

Important to remember, despite several blocks available in if..elif..else, only one block will be executed.

Example:

Three conditions are covered, but only one can execute at a given instance.

Start IDLE.

Navigate to the File menu and click New Window.

Type the following:

number_mine=87

if(number>0):

  print(number_mine, "This is a positive number")

elif(number_mie==0):

  print(number_mine, "The number is zero")

else:

  print(number_mine, "The number is a negative number")

Discussion:

There are three possibilities but at any given instance the only condition will exist and this qualifies the use of if family flow control statement.

For three or more conditions to evaluate, the if…elif..else flow statement merits.

Nested if Statements in Python

Sometimes, a condition exists, but there are more sub-conditions that need to be covered, which leads to a concept known as nesting.

The amount of statements to nests is not limited, but you should exercise caution as you will realize nesting can lead to user errors when writing code.

Nesting can also complicate maintaining of code.

The only indentation can help determine the level of nesting.

Example

Start IDLE.

Navigate to the File menu and click New Window.

Type the following:

my_charact=str(input("Type a character here either 'a', 'b' or 'c':"))

if (my_charact='a'):

  if(my_charact='a'):

    print("a")

else if:

  (my_charact='b')

  print("b")

else:

 print("c")

Practice Exercise

Write a program that uses the if..else flow control statement to check non-leap year and display either scenario.

Include comments and indentation to enhance the readability of the program.

For Loop in Python

Indentation is used to separate the body of for loop in Python.

Note: Simple linear list takes the following syntax:

Variable_name=[values separated by a comma]

Example

Start IDLE.

Navigate to the File menu and click New Window.

Type the following:

numbers=[12, 3,18,10,7,2,3,6,1]   #Variable name storing the list

sum=0   #Initialize sum before usage, very important

for cumulative in numbers: #Iterate over the list

sum=sum+cumulative

print("The sum is" ,sum)

Practice Exercise

Start IDLE.

Navigate to the File menu and click New Window.

Type the following:

Write a Python program that uses the for loop to sum the following lists.

- ☐ marks=[3, 8,19, 6,18,29,15]
- ☐ ages=[12,17,14,18,11,10,16]
- ☐ mileage=[15,67,89,123,76,83]
- ☐ cups=[7,10,3,5,8,16,13]

Range() Function in Python

The range function (range()) in Python can help generate numbers.

Remember, in programming, the first item is indexed 0.

Therefore, range(11) will generate numbers from 0 to 10.

Example

Start IDLE.

Navigate to the File menu and click New Window.

Type the following:

print(range(7))

The output will be 0,1,2,3,4,5,6

Practice Exercise:

Without writing and running a Python program, what will be the output for:

- ☐ range(16)

- ☐ range(8)

- ☐ range(4)

Using range() and len() and indexing

Practice Exercise

Write a Python program to iterate through the following list and include the message I listen to (each of the music genre).

Use the for loop, len() and range().

folders=['Rumba', 'House', 'Rock']

Using for Loop with Else

It is possible to include a for loop with anything else but as an option.

The else block will be executed if the items contained in the sequence are exhausted.

Example

Start IDLE.

Navigate to the File menu and click New Window.

Type the following:

marks=[12, 15,17]

for i in marks:

    print(i)

else:

    print("No items left")

Challenge:

Write a Python program that prints all prime numbers between 1 and 50.

While Loop in Python

In Python, the while loop is used to iterate over a block of program code as long as the test condition stays True.

The while loop is used in contexts where the user does not know the loop cycles required.

As earlier indicated, the while loop body is determined through indentation.

Example

Start IDLE.

Navigate to the File menu and click New Window.

Type the following:

Caution: Failing to include the value of the counter will lead to an infinite loop.

Practice Exercise

- Write a Python program that utilizes the while flow control statement to display the sum of all odd numbers from 1 to 10.

- Write a Python program that employs the while flow control statement to display the sum of all numbers from 11 to 21.

- Write a Python program that incorporates a while flow control statement to display the sum of all even numbers from 1 to 10.

Using While Loop with Else

If the condition is false and no break occurs, a while loop's else part runs.

Example

Start IDLE.

Navigate to the File menu and click New Window.

Type the following:

track = 0

while track< 4:

  print("Within the loop")

track = track + 1

else:

  print("Now within the else segment")

Python's Break and Continue

Let us use real-life analogy where we have to force a stop on iteration before it evaluates completely.

Think of when cracking/breaking passwords using a simple dictionary attack that loops through all possible character combinations; you will want the program to strike the password searched without completing it immediately.

Again, think of when recovering photos you accidentally deleted using recovery software, you will want the recovery to stop iterating through the files immediately it finds items within the specified range.

The break and continue statement in Python works similarly.

Example

Start IDLE.

Navigate to the File menu and click New Window.

Type the following:

for tracker in "bring":

　if tracker == "i":

　　break

　print(tracker)

print("The End")

Continue Statement in Python

When the continue statement is used, the interpreter skips the rest of the code inside a loop for the current iteration only and the loop does not terminate.

The loop continues with the next iteration.

The syntax of Python continue

continue

Example

Start IDLE.

Navigate to the File menu and click New Window.

Type the following:

for tracker in "bring":

  if tracker == "i":

    continue

  print(tracker)

print("Finished")

The output of this program will be:

b

r

n

g

Finished

Analogy: Assume that you are running data recovery software and have specified skip word files (.doc, dox extension).

The program will have to continue iterating even after skipping word files.

Practice Exercise

- Write a Python program using for loop that will break after striking "v" in the string "Oliver".

- Write a Python program that will continue after skipping "m" in the string "Lemon".

Pass Statement in Python

Like a comment, a pass statement does not impact the program as it leads to no operation.

The syntax of pass

pass

Think of a program code that you plan to use in the future but is not currently needed.

Instead of having to insert that code in the future, the code can be written as pass statements.

Example

Start IDLE.

Navigate to the File menu and click New Window.

Type the following:

my_list={'k','i','n'}

for tracker in my_list:

   pass

Functions in Python

Functions in Python help split large code into smaller units.

Functions make a program more organized and easy to manage.

In Python functions will assume the syntax form below:

def name_of_function (arguments):

   """docstring"""

statements(s)

Example

Start IDLE.

Navigate to the File menu and click New Window.

Type the following:

def welcome(salute):

"""The Python function welcomes you to the individual passed in as parameter"""

print("Welcome " + salute + ". Lovely Day!")

Calling a Function in Python

We can call a function once we have defined it from another function or program.

Calling a function simply involves typing the function name with suitable parameters.

Start IDLE.

Navigate to the File menu and click New Window.

Type the following:

welcome('Brenda')

The output will be "Welcome Brenda. Lovely Day!'

Practice Exercise

Write a function that when called outputs "Hello (student name), kindly submit your work by Sunday."

Docstring

It is placed after the function header as the first statement and explains in summary what the function does.

Docstring should always be placed between triple quotes to accommodate multiple line strings.

Calling/Invoking the docstring we typed earlier

Example

Start IDLE.

Navigate to the File menu and click New Window.

Type the following:

print(welcome._doc_)

The output will be "This function welcomes you to

the individual passed in as

parameter".

The syntax for calling/invoking the docstring is:

print(function_name. _doc_)

Python Function Return Statement

Return syntax

return [list of expressions]

Discussion

The return statement can return a value or a None object.

Example

Print(welcome("Richard"))   #Passing arguments and calling the function

Welcome, Richard. Lovely Day!

None   #the returned value

Random Function in Python

Start IDLE.

Navigate to the File menu and click New Window.

Type the following:

import math

print(random.shuffle_num(11, 21))

y=['f','g','h','m']

print(random.pick(y))

random.anypic(y)

print(y)

print(your_pick.random())

Iterators

In Python, iterator refers to objects that can be iterated upon.

The for loop is used to implement iterators in Python anywhere.

Iterators in Python can also be implemented using generators and comprehensions.

In Python, an iterator concerns a construct that can be called several times performing the same action.

Iterators in Python implement the _iter_() special method and _next_() special method, which is collectively referred to as the iterator protocol.

In Python, an object becomes iterable if we can get an iterator from it, for example, string, tuple, and the list is iterable.

In operation, the iter() function calls the _iter_() method and returns an iterator from the set or list or string.

Manually Iterating Through Items in Python

The next() function is used in Python to manually loop through all the items of an iterator

Example

list_mine = [14, 17, 10, 13]

iter_list = iter(list_mine)

print(next(iter_list))

print(next(iter_list))

print(my_iter.__next__())

print(my_iter.__next__())

next(iter_list)

NOTE

The for loop provides an efficienty ay of automatically iterating through a list.

The for loop can be applied on a file, list or string among others
in Python.

Example

for element in list_mine:

  print(element)

Explaining the Loop

The for loop gets to iterate automatically through the Python
list.

Example

for element in list_mine:

object_iter = iter(iterable)

while True:

  try:

    element = next(object_iter)

  except StopIteration:

    break

Creating Custom Iterator in Python

On the other hand, the _next_() will scan and give the next element in the sequence and will trigger the StopIteration exception once it reaches the end.

Example

class Power:

  """Will implement powers of 2

  """

  def __init__(self, max = 0):

    self.max = max

  def __iter__(self):

    self.m = 0

    return self

  def __next__(self):

    if self.m <= self.max:

      *result = 2 ** self.m*

      self.m += 1

      return result

else:

   raise StopIteration

Discussion

Example

for j in Power(5):

   print(j)

Infinite Iterators

There may be situations that require continuous iteration.

The situations we have tackled so far were infinite iterators and had to terminate after exhausting the items in the iterable.

The iter() is an inbuilt function.

The method is fired by providing two arguments.

The first argument in iter() is the one being called while the other argument acts as a sentinel.

Until the function returns a value equal to the Sentinel, the iterator will continue calling the function.

Example

int()

infer = iterate(int,2)

next(infer)

next(infer)

Discussion

The int() function in this program will always return value 0.

Therefore, passing the function as iterate(int, 2) will return an iterator that invokes int().

The calling of int() will stop when the returned value equals 2.

Since this will never happen, we will end up with an infinite iterator.

Example

Assume we want to display all odd numbers that exist.

Practice Exercise

Write a Python program that uses a custom infinite iterator to display all even numbers.

Closure Function in Python

Example

def printing(msg):

  def printers():

    print(msg)

  return printer

custom = printing("Welcome")

custom()

Discussion

The printing() function was invoked with the string "Welcome" that gives us objects associated with the name.

Calling custom() implied the message was remembered even though it had already completed executing the printing() function.

In Python, the technique via which part of the data gets tied to the code is termed closure.

In this case, even when the variable gets out of scope, the value in the enclosing scope is remembered.

Example

del printing

another()

printing("Welcome")

NOTE

In Python, closures help provide a limited form of encapsulation.

The use of enclosures can help avoid the wide usage of global scope variables.

Remember, global scope implies that the names are accessible and modifiable at any part of the program, which can create inconsistency.

Closures can also be used to give an object-oriented solution to a problem.

Example

def product(n):

  def times(y):

    return y* number

  return times

multiply1 = times(13)

multiply1 = times(15)

print(multiply2(19))

print(multiply2(13))

print(multiply2(multiply(12)))

Projects - Implementing Simple Calculator in Python

def sum(m, n):

   return m + n

def minus(m, n):

   return m - n

def product(m, n):

   return m * n

def division(m, n):

   return m / n

print("Choose an Operation.")

```python
print("1.Sum")

print("2.Minus")

print("3.Product")

print("4.Division")

option = input("Type your choice (1/2/3/4):")

number1 = int(input("Enter number 1: "))

number2 = int(input("Enter number 2: "))

if option == '1':

    print(number1,"+",number2,"=", sum(number1,number2))

elif option == '2':

    print(number1,"-",number2,"=", minus(num1,num2))

elif choice == '3':

    print(number1,"*",number2,"=", product(number1,number2))

elif choice == '4':

    print(number1,"/",number2,"=", division(number1,number2))

else:
```

```
    print("Check Your Selection, Out of Range")
```

Program to return factors of any integer

```
def factors(m):

    print("We found factors of",m,"as:")

    for j in range(1, m + 1):

        if m % j == 0:

            print(j)

number = 400

factors(number)
```

Chapter 5. Exception Handling

What Is Exception Handling?

Exception handling is error management.

It has three purposes:

- It allows you to debug your program.

- It allows your program to continue running despite encountering an error or exception.

- It allows you to create your customized errors that can help you debug, remove, and control some of Python's nuances and make your program function as you want it to.

Handling the Zero Division Error Exception

Exception handling can be an easy or difficult task depending on how you want your program to flow and your creativity.

You might have scratched your head because of the word creativity.

Programming is all about logic, right? No.

The core purpose of programming is to solve problems.

A solution to a problem does not only require logic.

It also requires creativity.

Have you ever heard of the phrase, "Think outside of the box?"

Program breaking exceptions can be a pain, and they are often called bugs.

The solution to such problems is often elusive.

And you need to find a workaround or risk rewriting your program from scratch.

For example, you have a calculator program with this snippet of code when you divide:

```
>>> def div(dividend, divisor):
        print(dividend / divisor)
>>> div(7, 0)
Traceback (recent call to come last):
  File "<stdin>", line 1, in <module>
  File "<stdin>", line 2, in div
ZeroDivisionError: division by zero
```

```
>>> _
```

Of course, division by zero is an impossible operation.

Because of that, Python stops the program since it does not know what you want to do when this is encountered.

It does not know any valid answer or response.

That being said, the problem here is that the error stops your program entirely.

To manage this exception, you have two options.

First, you can make sure to prevent such an operation from happening in your program.

Second, you can let the operation and errors happen, but tell Python to continue your program.

Here is what the first solution looks like:

```
>>> def div(dividend, divisor):
    if (divisor != 0):
        print(dividend / divisor)
    else:
        print("Cannot Divide by Zero.")
```

```
>>> div(5, 0)
```

Cannot Divide by Zero.

```
>>> _
```

Here is what the second solution looks like:

```
>>> def div(dividend, divisor):
        try:
            print(dividend / divisor)
        except:
            print("Cannot Divide by Zero.")
>>> div(5, 0)
```

Cannot Divide by Zero.

```
>>> _
```

Remember the two core solutions to errors and exceptions.

One, prevent the error from happening.

Two, manage the aftermath of the error.

Using Try-Except Blocks

In the previous example, the try-except blocks were used to *manage* the error.

However, you or your user can still do something to screw your solution up.

For example:

>>> def div(dividend, divisor):

    try:

        print(dividend / divisor)

    except:

        print("Cannot Divide by Zero.")

>>> div(5, "a")

Cannot Divide by Zero.

>>> _

The statement prepared for the "except" block is not enough to justify the error that was created by the input.

Dividing a number by a string does not actually warrant a "Cannot Divide by Zero." message.

For this to work, you need to know more about how to use except block properly.

First of all, you can specify the error that it will capture and respond to by indicating the exact exception.

For example:

>>> def div(dividend, divisor):

    try:

        print(dividend / divisor)

    except ZeroDivisionError:

        print("Cannot Divide by Zero.")

>>> div(5, 0)

Cannot Divide by Zero.

>>> div(5, "a")

Traceback (most recent call last):

  File "<stdin>", line 1, <module>

  File "<stdin>", line 3, in div

TypeError: unsupported operand type(s) for /: 'int' and 'str'

\>\>\> _

Now, the error that will be handled has been specified.

When the program encounters the specified error, it will execute the statements written on the "except" block that captured it.

If no except block is set to capture other errors, Python will then step in, stop the program, and give you an exception.

But why did that happen?

When the example did not specify the error, it handled everything.

That is correct.

When the "except" block does not have any specified error to look out for, it will capture any error instead.

For example:

\>\>\> def div(dividend, divisor):

    try:

        print(dividend / divisor)

    except:

        print("An error happened.")

\>>> div(5, 0)

An error happened.

\>>> div(5, "a")

An error happened.

\>>> _

That is a better way of using the "except" block if you do not know exactly the error that you might encounter.

Reading an Exception Error Trace Back

The most important part in error handling is to know how to read the trace-back message.

It is fairly easy to do.

The trace-back message is structured like this:

<Traceback Stack Header>

   <File Name>, <Line Number>, <Function/Module>

<Exception>: <Exception Description>

Here are things you need to remember:

- The traceback stack header informs you that an error occurred.

- The filename tells you the name of the file where the fault is located.

Since the book's examples are coded using the interpreter, it always indicated that the file name is "<stdin>" or standard input.

- The line number tells the exact line number in the file that caused the error.

Since the examples are tested in the interpreter, it will always say line 1.

However, if the error is found in a code block or module, it will return the line number of the statement relative to the code block or module.

- The function/module part tells what function or module owns the statement.

If the code block does not have an identifier or the statement is declared outside code blocks, it will default to <module>.

- The exception tells you what kind of error happened.

Some of them are built-in classes (e.g., ZeroDivisionError, TypeError, and etcetera) while some are just errors (e.g., SyntaxError).

You can use them on your except blocks.

- The exception description gives you more details with regards to how the error occurred.

The description format may vary from error to error.

Using Exceptions to Prevent Crashes

Anyway, to know the exceptions that you can use, all you need to do is to generate the error.

For example, using the TypeError found in the previous example, you can capture that error too and provide the correct statements in response.

```
>>> def div(dividend, divisor):
    try:
        print(dividend / divisor)
    except ZeroDivisionError:
        print("Cannot Divide by Zero.")
```

    except TypeError:

        print("Cannot Divide by Anything Other Than a Number.")

    except:

        print("An unknown error has been detected.")

\>>> div(5, 0)

Cannot Divide by Zero.

\>>> div(5, "a")

Cannot Divide by Anything Other Than a Number.

\>>> div(undeclaredVariable / 20)

An unknown error has been detected.

\>>> _

However, catching errors this way can still be problematic.

It allows you to prevent a crash or stop, but you have no idea about what happened.

To know the unknown error, you can use the **as** keyword to pass the Exception details to a variable.

Convention wise, the variable detail is often used for this purpose.

For example:

```
>>> def div(dividend, divisor):
    try:
        print(dividend / divisor)
    except Exception as detail:
        print("An error has been detected.")
        print(detail)
        print("Continuing with the program.")
>>> div(5, 0)
An error has been detected.
division by zero
Continuing with the program.
>>> div(5, "a")
An error has been detected.
unsupported operand type(s) for /: 'int' and 'str'
```

Continuing with the program.

>>> _

The Else Block

There are times that an error happens in the middle of your code block.

You can catch that error with try and except.

However, you might not want to execute any statement in that code block if an error happens.

For example:

>>> def div(dividend, divisor):

    try:

        quotient = dividend / divisor

    except Exception as detail:

        print("An error has been detected.")

        print(detail)

        print("Continuing with the program.")

        print(str(dividend) + " divided by " + str(divisor) + " is:")

```
    print(quotient)
>>> div(4, 2)
4 divided by 2 is:
2.0
>>> div(5, 0)
An error has been detected.
division by zero
Continuing with the program.
5 divided by 0 is:
Traceback (most recent call last):
  File "<stdin>", line 1, in <module>
  File "<stdin>", line 8, in div
    Print(quotient)
UnboundLocalError: local variable 'quotient' referenced before assignment
>>> _
```

As you can see, the next statements after the initial fault are dependent on it thus, they are also affected.

In this example, the variable quotient returned an error when used after the try and except block since its supposed value was not assigned because the expression assigned to it was impossible to evaluate.

In this case, you would want to drop the remaining statements that are dependent on the contents of the try clause.

To do that, you must use the else block.

For example:

>>> def div(dividend, divisor):

  try:

      quotient = dividend / divisor

  except Exception as detail:

      print("An error has been detected.")

      print(detail)

      print("Continuing with the program.")

```
    else:

        print(str(dividend) + " divided by " + str(divisor) + " is:")

        print(quotient)
>>> div(4, 2)
```

4 divided by 2 is:

2

```
>>> div(5, 0)
```

An error has been detected.

division by zero

Continuing with the program.

```
>>> _
```

The first attempt on using the function with proper arguments went well.

On the second attempt, the program did not execute the last two statements under the else block because it returned an error.

The else block always follows except blocks.

The else block's function is to let Python execute the statements under it when the try block did not return and let Python ignore them if an exception happens.

Failing Silently

Failing silently or silent fails is a programming term often used during error and exception handling.

From a user's perspective, silent failure is a state wherein a program fails at a certain point but never informs a user.

From a programmer's perspective, silent failure is a state wherein the parser, runtime development environment, or compiler fails to produce an error or exception and proceed with the program.

This often leads to unintended results.

A programmer can also induce silent failures when he either ignores exceptions or bypasses them.

Alternatively, he blatantly hides them and creates workarounds to make the program operate as expected, even if an error happened.

He might do that because of multiple reasons, such as the error is not program breaking or the user does not need to know about the error.

Handling the File Not Found Exception Error

There will be times when you will encounter the FileNotFoundError.

Handling such an error depends on your intent or purpose with regards to opening the file.

Here are common reasons you will encounter this error:

- You did not pass the directory and filename as a string.
- You misspelled the directory and filename.
- You did not specify the directory.
- You did not include the correct file extension.
- The file does not exist.

The first method to handle the FileNotFoundError exception is to make sure that all the common reasons do not cause it.

Once you do, then you will need to choose the best way to handle the error, which is completely dependent on the reason you are opening a file in the first place.

Checking If File Exists

Again, there are always two ways to handle an exception: preventive and reactive.

The preventive method is to check if the file exists in the first place.

To do that, you will need to use the os (os.py) module that comes with your Python installation.

Then, you can use its path module's isfile() function.

The path module's file name depends on the operating system (posixpath for UNIX, ntpath for Windows, macpath for old MacOS).

For example:

>>> from os import path

>>> path.isfile("random.txt")

False

>>> path.isfile("sampleFile.txt")

True

>>> _

Try and Except

You can also do it the hard way by using try, except, and else blocks.

```
>>> def openFile(filename):
    try:
        x = open(filename, "r")
    except FileNotFoundError:
        print("The file '" + filename + "' does not exist.")
    except FileNotFound:
        print("The file '" + filename + "' does exist.")
>>> openFile("random.txt")
The file 'random.txt' does not exist.
>>> openFile("sampleFile.txt")
The file 'sampleFile.txt' does exist.
>>> _
```

Creating a New File

If the file does not exist, and your goal is to overwrite any existing file anyway, then it will be best for you to use the "w" or "w+" access mode.

The access mode creates a new file for you if it does not exist.

For example:

>>> x = open("new.txt", "w")

>>> x.tell()

0

>>> _

If you are going to read and write, use "w+" access mode instead.

Chapter 6. Variable Scope and Lifetime in Python Functions

Variables and parameters defined within a Python function have local scope implying they are not visible from outside.

In Python, the variable lifetime is valid as long the function executes and is the period throughout that a variable exists in memory.

Returning the function destroys the function variables.

Example:

Start IDLE.

Navigate to the File menu and click New Window.

Type the following:

def function_my()

  marks=15

print("The value inside the function is:", marks)

marks=37

function_my()

Print"The value outside the function is:",marks)

Function Types

They are broadly grouped into user-defined and built-in functions.

The built-in functions are part of the Python interpreter while the user specifies the user-defined functions.

Exercise:

Give three examples of built-in functions in Pythons.

Function Argument

Calling a function requires passing the correct number of parameters; otherwise, the interpreter will generate an error.

Illustration

Start IDLE.

Navigate to the File menu and click New Window.

Type the following:

def salute(name,message):

   """This function welcomes to

the student with the provided message"""

  print("Welcome",salute + ', ' + message)

welcome("Brenda","Lovely Day!")

Note: the function welcome() has two parameters.

We will not get any error as it has been fed with two arguments.

Let us try calling the function with one argument and see what happens:

welcome("Brenda")   #only one argument passed

Running this program will generate an error saying "TypeError: welcome() missing 1 required positional argument.

The same will happen when we pass no arguments to the function.

Example 2:

Start IDLE.

Navigate to the File menu and click New Window.

Type the following:

welcome()

The interpreter will generate an error "typeerror: welcome() missing 2 required positional arguments".

Keywords Arguments in Python

Python provides a way of calling functions using keyword arguments.

When calling functions using keyword arguments, the order of arguments can be changed.

The values of a function are matched to the argument position-wise.

Note:

In the previous example, function welcome when invoked as welcome("Brenda," "Lovely Day!").

The value "Brenda" is assigned to the argument name and "Lovely Day!" to msg.

Calling the function using keywords

Start IDLE.

Navigate to the File menu and click New Window.

Type the following:

welcome(name="Brenda", msg="Lovely Day!")

Keywords not following the order

Welcome(msg="Lovely Day!", name="Brenda")

Arbitrary Arguments

It may happen that we do not have knowledge of all arguments needed to be passed into a function.

Analogy: assume that you are writing a program to welcome all new students this semester.

In this case, you do not how many will report.

Example

Start IDLE.

Navigate to the File menu and click New Window.

Type the following:

def welcome(*names):

"""This welcome function salutes all students in the names tuple."""

   for name in names:

print("Welcome".name)

welcome("Lucy","Richard","Fridah","James")

The output of the program will be:

Welcome Lucy

Welcome Richard

Welcome Fridah

Welcome James

Recursion in Python

The definition of something in terms of itself is called recursion.

A recursive function calls other functions.

Example:

Python program to compute integer factorials

Start IDLE.

Navigate to the File menu and click New Window.

Type the following:

Exercise

Write a Python program to find the factorial of 7.

Python Anonymous Function

Some functions may be specified devoid of a name, and these are called anonymous functions.

The lambda keyword is used to denote an anonymous function.

Anonymous functions are also referred to as lambda functions in Python.

Syntax

lambda arguments: expression.

Lambda functions must always have one expression but can have several arguments.

Example:

Start IDLE.

Navigate to the File menu and click New Window.

Type the following:

double = lambda y: y * 2

Output: 10

print(double(5))

Example 2:

We can use inbuilt functions such as filter () and lambda to show only even numbers in a list/tuple.

Start IDLE.

Navigate to the File menu and click New Window.

Type the following:

first_marks = [3, 7, 14, 16, 18, 21, 13, 32]

fresh_marks = list(filter(lambda n: (n%2 == 0) , first_marks))

Output: [14, 16, 18, 32]

print(fresh_marks)

Lambda function and map() can be used to double individual list items.

Example 3:

Start IDLE.

Navigate to the File menu and click New Window.

Type the following:

first_score = [3, 7, 14, 16, 18, 21, 13, 32]

fresh_score = list(map(lambda m: m * 2 , first_score))

Output: [6, 14, 28, 32, 36, 42, 26, 64]

Print(fresh_score)

Python's Global, Local and Nonlocal

Python's Global Variables

Variables declared outside of a function in Python are known as global variables.

They are declared in the global scope.

A global variable can be accessed outside or inside of the function.

Example:

Start IDLE.

Navigate to the File menu and click New Window.

Type the following:

y= "global"

def foo():

    print("y inside the function :", y)

foo()

print("y outside the function:", y)

Explanation:

In the illustration above, y is a global variable and is defined as a foo() to print the global variable y.

When we call the foo() it will print the value of y.

Local Variables:

 A local variable is declared within the body of the function or in the local scope.

Example:

Start IDLE.

Navigate to the File menu and click New Window.

Type the following:

def foo():

    x = "local"

foo()

print(x)

Explanation:

Running this program will generate an error indicating 'x' is undefined.

The error is occurring because we are trying to access local variable x in a global scope, whereas foo() functions only in the local scope.

Creating a Local Variable in Python

Example:

A local variable is created by declaring a variable within the function.

def foo():

Start IDLE.

Navigate to the File menu and click New Window.

Type the following:

    x = "local"

    print(x)

foo()

Explanation:

When we execute the code, the output will be:

Local

Python's Global and Local Variable

Using both local and global variables in the same code.

Example:

Start IDLE.

Navigate to the File menu and click New Window.

Type the following:

y = "global"

def foo():

    global y

    x = "local"

    y = y * 2

    print(y)

    print(x)

foo()

Explanation:

The output of the program will be:

global global

local

Explanation:

We declared y as a global variable and x as a local variable in the foo().

The * operator issued to modify the global variable y, and finally, we printed both y and x.

Local and Global Variables with the same name

Start IDLE.

Navigate to the File menu and click New Window.

Type the following:

y=6

def foo():

y=11

print("Local variable y-", y)

foo()

Print("Global variable y-", y)

Python's Nonlocal Variables

A Python's nonlocal variable is used in a nested function whose local scope is unspecified.

It is neither global nor local scope.

Example:

Creating a nonlocal variable.

Start IDLE.

Navigate to the File menu and click New Window.

Type the following:

def outer():

  y = "local variable"

  def inner():

    nonlocal y

    y = "nonlocal variable"

```
    print("inner:", y)

  inner()

  print("outer scope:", y)

Outer()
```

Global Keyword in Python

There are rules when creating a global keyword:

A global keyword is local by default when we create a variable within a function.

It is global by default when we define a variable outside of a function, and you do not need to use the global keyword.

The global keyword is used to read and write a global variable within a function.

The use of a global keyword outside a function will have no effect.

Example:

Start IDLE.

Navigate to the File menu and click New Window.

Type the following:

```
number = 3      #A global variable

def add():

    print(number)

add()
```

The output of this program will be 3.

Modifying a global variable from inside the function.

```
number=3           #a global variable

def add():

    number= number + 4    # add 4 to 3

    print(number)

add()
```

Explanation:

When the program is executed it will generate an error indicating that the local variable number is referenced before assignment.

The reason for encountering the error is that we can only access the global variable but cannot modify it from inside the function.

Using a global keyword would solve this.

Example:

Start IDLE.

Navigate to the File menu and click New Window.

Type the following:

Modifying global variable within a function using the global keyword.

number = 3   # a global variable

def add():

   global number

   number= number + 1 # increment by 1

   print("Inside the function add():", number)

add()

print("In main area:", number)

Explanation:

When the program is run, the output will be:

Inside the function add(): 4

In the main area: 4

We defined a number as a global keyword within the function add().

The variable was then incremented by 1, variable number.

Then we called the add () function to print global variable c.

Creating Global Variables across Python Modules

We can create a single module config.py that will contain all global variables and share the information across several modules within the same program.

Example:

Start IDLE.

Navigate to the File menu and click New Window.

Type the following:

Create config.py

x=0

y="empty"

Then create an update.py file to modify global variables

Import config

config.x=11

config.y="Today"

Then create a main.py file to evaluate the changes in value

import config

import update

print(config.x)

print(config.y)

Explanation

Running the main.py file will generate:

11

Today

Python Modules

Modules consist of definitions as well as program statements.

An illustration is a file name config.py, which is considered as a module.

The module name would be config.

Modules are used to help break large programs into smaller, manageable, and organized files, as well as promoting the reusability of code.

Example: Creating the First module

Start IDLE.

Navigate to the File menu and click New Window.

Type the following:

Def add(x, y):

""""This is a program to add two

  numbers and return the outcome""""

outcome=x+y

return outcome

Module Import

The keyword import is used to import.

Example:

Import first

The dot operator can help us access a function as long as we know the module's name.

Example:

Start IDLE.

Navigate to the File menu and click New Window.

Type the following:

first.add(6,8)

Explanation:

Import Statement in Python

The import statement can be used to access the definitions within a module via the dot operator.

Start IDLE.

Navigate to the File menu and click New Window.

Type the following:

import math

print("The PI value is", math.pi)

Import with renaming

Example:

Start IDLE.

Navigate to the File menu and click New Window.

Type the following:

import math as h

   print("The PI value is-",h.pi)

Explanation:

In this case, h is our renamed math module with a view helping save typing time in some instances.

When we rename, the new name becomes valid and recognized one and not the original one.

From...import statement Python.

It is possible to import particular names from a module rather than importing the entire module.

Example:

Start IDLE.

Navigate to the File menu and click New Window.

Type the following:

from math import pi

Print("The PI value is-", pi)

Importing All Names

Example:

Start IDLE.

Navigate to the File menu and click New Window.

Type the following:

from math import*

print("The PI value is-", pi)

Explanation:

In this context, we are importing all definitions from a particular module, but it is an encouraging norm as it can lead to unseen duplicates.

Module Search Path in Python

Example:

Start IDLE.

Navigate to the File menu and click New Window.

Type the following:

import sys

sys.path

Python searches everywhere, including the sys file.

Reloading a Module

Python will only import a module once, increasing efficiency in execution.

print("This program was executed")

import mine

Reloading Code

Example:

Start IDLE.

Navigate to the File menu and click New Window.

Type the following:

import mine

import mine

import mine

Mine.reload(mine)

Dir() built-in Python function

For discovering names contained in a module, we use the dir() inbuilt function.

Syntax

Dir(module_name)

Python Package

Files in python hold modules and directories are stored in packages.

A single package in Python holds similar modules.

Therefore, different modules should be placed in different Python packages.

Data types in Python

- ☐ Numbers

The presence or absence of a decimal point separates integers and floating points.

For instance, 4 is an integer, while 4.0 is a floating-point number.

On the other hand, complex numbers in Python are denoted as r+tj, where j represents the real part, and t is the virtual part.

In this context, the function type() is used to determine the variable class.

The Python function instance() is invoked to make a determination of which specific class function originates from.

Example:

Start IDLE.

Navigate to the File menu and click New Window.

Type the following:

number=6

print(type(number))#should output class int

print(type(6.0))#should output class float

complex_num=7+5j

print(complex_num+5)

print(isinstance(complex_num, complex))#should output True

Important: Integers in Python can be of infinite length.

Floating numbers in Python are assumed precise up to fifteen decimal places.

Number Conversion

This segment assumes you have prior basic knowledge of how to manually or using a calculator to convert decimal into binary, octal, and hexadecimal.

Check out the Windows Calculator in Windows 10, Calculator version Version 10.1804.911.1000, and choose programmer mode to convert automatically.

Programmers often need to convert decimal numbers into octal, hexadecimal, and binary forms.

A prefix in Python allows the denotation of these numbers to their corresponding type.

Number SystemPrefix

Octal'oO' or 'oo'

Binary'oB' or 'ob'

Hexadecimal'0X or '0x'

Example:

print(0b1010101)#Output:85

print(0x7B+0b0101)#Output: 128 (123+5)

print(0o710)#Output:710

Exercise:

Write a Python program to display the following:

a.0011 11112

b.7478

C.9316

Type Conversion

Sometimes referred to as coercion, type conversion allows us to change one type of number into another.

The preloaded functions such as float(), int() and complex() enable implicit and explicit type conversions.

The same functions can be used to change from strings.

Example

Start IDLE.

Navigate to the File menu and click New Window.

Type the following:

int(5.3)#Gives 5

int(5.9)#Gives 5

The int() will produce a truncation effect when applied to floating numbers.

It will simply drop the decimal point part without rounding off.

For the float() let us take a look:

Start IDLE.

Navigate to the File menu and click New Window.

Type the following:

float(6)#Gives 6.0

ccomplex('4+2j')#Gives (4+2j)

Exercise:

Apply the int() conversion to the following:

a. 4.1

b.4.7

c.13.3

d.13.9

Apply the float() conversion to the following:

e.7

f.16

G.19

☐   *Decimal in Python*

Example:

Start IDLE.

Navigate to the File menu and click New Window.

Type the following:

(1.2+2.1)==3.3 #Will return False, why?

Explanation:

The computer works with finite numbers, and fractions cannot be stored in their raw form as they will create an infinitely long binary sequence.

☐ *Fractions in Python*

The fractions module in Python allows operations on fractional numbers.

Example:

Start IDLE.

Navigate to the File menu and click New Window.

Type the following:

import fractions

print(fractions.my_fraction(2.5))#Output 5/2

print(fractions.my_fraction(4))#Output 5

print(fractions.my_fraction(2,5))#output 2/5

Important:

Creating my_fraction from float can lead to unusual results due to the misleading representation of binary floating point.

Mathematics in Python

To carry out mathematical functions, Python offers modules like random and math.

Start IDLE.

Navigate to the File menu and click New Window.

Type the following:

import math

print(math.pi)#output:3.14159....

print(math.cos(math.pi))#the output will be -1.0

print(math.exp(10))#the output will be 22026.4....

print(math.log10(100))#the output will be 2

print(math.factorial(5))#the output will be 120

Exercise:

Write a python program that uses math functions from the math module to perform the following:

a.Square of 34

b.Log1010000

c.Cos 45 x sin 90

D.Exponent of 20

Random Function in Python

Start IDLE.

Navigate to the File menu and click New Window.

Type the following:

import math

print(random.shuffle_num(11, 21))

y=['f','g','h','m']

print(random.pick(y))

random.anypic(y)

print(y)

Print(your_pick.random())

Lists in Python

We create a list in Python by placing items called elements inside square brackets separated by commas.

The items in a list can be of mixed data types.

Start IDLE.

Navigate to the File menu and click New Window.

Type the following:

list_mine=[]#empty list

list_mine=[2,5,8]#list of integers

list_mine=[5,"Happy", 5.2]#list having mixed data types

Exercise:

Write a program that captures the following in a list: "Best", 26,89,3.9

Nested Lists

A nested list is a list as an item in another list.

Example:

Start IDLE.

Navigate to the File menu and click New Window.

Type the following:

list_mine=["carrot", [9, 3, 6], ['g']]

Exercise

Write a nested for the following elements: [36,2,1],"Writer",'t',[3.0, 2.5]

Accessing Elements from a List

In programming and in Python specifically, the first time is always indexed zero.

For a list of five items, we will access them from index0 to index4.

Failure to access the items in a list in this manner will create an index error.

The index is always an integer as using other number types will create a type error.

For nested lists, they are accessed via nested indexing.

Example:

Start IDLE.

Navigate to the File menu and click New Window.

Type the following:

list_mine=['b','e','s','t']

print(list_mine[0])#the output will be b

print(list_mine[2])#the output will be s

print(list_mine[3])#the output will be t

Exercise:

Given the following list:

your_collection=['t','k','v','w','z','n','f']

a.Write a Python program to display the second item in the list

b.Write a Python program to display the sixth item in the last

C.Write a Python program to display the last item in the list.

Chapter 7. Modules

What Are the Modules?

In Python, a module is a portion of a program (an extension file) that can be invoked through other programs without having to write them in every program used.

Besides, they can define classes and variables.

These modules contain related sentences between them and can be used at any time.

The modules' use is based on using a code (program body, functions, and variables) already stored on it called import.

With the use of the modules, it can be observed that Python allows simplifying the programs a lot because it allows us to simplify the problems into a smaller one to make the code shorter so that programmers do not get lost when looking for something in hundreds of coding lines when making codes.

How to Create a Module?

To create a module in Python, we don't need a lot; it's very simple.

For example: if you want to create a module that prints a city, we write our code in the editor and save it as "mycity.py"

Once this is done, we will know that this will be our module's name (omitting the .py sentence), which will be assigned to the global variable __city__.

This is a very simple code designed for users of Python 2.

The print function is not in parentheses, so that's the way this Python version handles that function.

But, beyond that, we can see that the file "mycity.py" is pretty simple and not complicated at all, since the only thing inside is a function called "print_city," which will have a string as a parameter, and what it will do is to print "Hello, welcome to," and this will concatenate with the string that was entered as a parameter.

Import Statement

This statement is used to import a module.

Through any Python code file, its process is as follows:

- The Python interpreter searches the file system for the current directory where it is executed.

- Then, the interpreter searches for its predefined paths in its configuration.

- When it meets the first match (the module's name), the interpreter automatically executes it from start to finish.

When importing a module for the first time, Python will generate a compiled .pyc extension file.

This extension file will be used in the following imports of this module.

When the interpreter detects that the module has already been modified since the last time it was generated, it will generate a new module.

Example:

This will print:

You must save the imported file in the same directory where Python is using the import statement so that Python can find it.

As we could see in our example, importing a module allows us to improve our program's functionalities through external files.

Now, let's see some examples. The first one is a calculator where will create a module that performs all the mathematical functions and another program that runs the calculator itself.

The first thing we do is the module "calculator.py" which is responsible for doing all the necessary operations.

Among them are addition, subtraction, division, and multiplication, as you can see.

We included the use of conditional statements such as if, else, and elif.

We also included the use of exceptions so that the program will not get stuck every time the user enters an erroneous value at the numbers of the calculator for the division.

After that, we will create a program that will have to import the module previously referred to so that it manages to do all the pertinent mathematical functions.

But at this time, you might be thinking that the only existing modules are the ones that the programmer creates.

The answer is no since Python has modules that come integrated into it.

With them, we will make two more programs: the first one is an improvement of the one that we have just done, and the second one will be an alarm that will print on screen a string periodically.

First example:

The first thing that was done was to create the module, but at first sight, we have a surprise, which is that math was imported.

What does that mean to us?

Well, that we are acquiring the properties of the math module that comes by default in Python.

We see that the calculator function is created that has several options.

If the op value is equal to 1, the addition operation is made.

If it is equal to 2, the subtraction operation is made, and so on.

But so new is from op is equal to 5 because, if this is affirmative, then it will return the value of the square root of the values num1 and num2 through the use of math.sqrt(num1), which returns the result of the root.

Then, if op is equal to 6, using functions "math.radians()" which means that num1 or num2 will become radians since that is the type of value accepted by the functions "math.sin()," meaning that the value of the sin of num1 and num2 will return to us, which will be numbers entered by users arbitrarily who will become radians and then the value of the corresponding sin.

The last thing will be to create the main program, as it can be seen next:

Here, we can see the simple program, since it only imports the module "calculator.py," then the variables num1 and num2 are assigned the value by using an input.

Finally, an operation to do is chosen, and to finish is called the calculator function of the calculator module to which we will pass three parameters.

Second example:

We are going to create a module, which has within itself a function that acts as a chronometer in such a way that it returns true in case time ends.

In this module, as you can see, another module is imported, which is called "time," and as its name refers, functions to operate with times, and has a wide range of functions, from returning dates and times to help to create chronometers, among others.

The first thing we do is to create the cron() function, which starts declaring that the start Alarm variables will be equal to time.time, which means that we are giving an initial value to this function o know the exact moment in which the function was initialized to then enter into an infinite cycle.

Since the restriction is always True, therefore, this cycle will never end, unless the break command is inside it.

Then, within the while cycle, there are several instructions.

The first is that the final variable is equal to time.time() to consider the specific moment we are located and monitor time.

After that, another variable is created called times, and this acquires the value of the final minus start Alarm.

But you will be wondering what the round function does.

It rounds up the values; we do that to work easier.

But this is not enough; therefore, we use an if since, if the subtraction between the end and the beginning is greater or equal to 60, then one minute was completed, and what happens to this?

Why 60?

This is because the time module works with a second and for a minute to elapse, 60 seconds have to be elapsed. Therefore, the subtraction between the end and the beginning has to be greater than or equal to 60. True will be returned in the affirmative case, and finally, we will get out of the infinite cycle.

Once the alarm module is finished, we proceed to make the program, as we can see below:

We can see that the program imports two modules, the one we have created, the alarm and the time module.

The first thing we do is to create the variable s as an input, which tells the user if he wants to start.

If the answer is affirmative, then the variable h representing the time will be equal to "time.strftime ("%H:%M:%S")," which means that we are using a function of the time module that returns the hour to use in the specified format so that it can then be printed using the print function.

The next action is to use the alarm module using the command alarm.cron(), which means that the cron() function is being called.

When this function is finished, the time will be assigned to the variable h, again, to finish printing it and being able to observe its correct operation.

As a conclusion of this chapter, we can say that the modules are fundamental for the proper performance of the programmer since they allow to make the code more legible, in addition, that it allows subdividing the problems to attack them from one to one and thus to carry out the tasks easily.

Locate a Module

When importing a module, the interpreter automatically searches the same module for its current address, if this is not available, Python (or its interpreter) will perform a search on the

PYTHONPATH environment variable that is nothing more than a list containing directory names with the same syntax as the environment variable.

If in any particular case, these previous actions failed, Python would look for a default UNIX path (located in /user/local/lib/python on Windows).

The modules are searched in the directory list given by the variable sys.path.

This variable contains the current directory, the PYTHONPATH directory, and the entire directory that comes by default in the installation.

Syntax of PYTHONPATH

A PYTHONPATH syntax made in windows looks like this:

Unlike a PYTHONPATH syntax made in UNIX

Chapter 8. Working with Files

Programs are made with input and output in mind.

You input data to the program, the program processes the input, and it ultimately provides you with output.

For example, a calculator will take in numbers and operations you want.

It will then process the operation you wanted.

And then, it will display the result to you as its output.

There are multiple ways for a program to receive input and to produce output.

One of those ways is to read and write data on files.

To start learning how to work with files, you need to learn the open() function.

The open() function has one *required* parameter and two *optional* parameters.

The first and required parameter is the file name.

The second parameter is the access mode.

And the third parameter is buffering or buffer size.

The filename parameter requires string data.

The access mode requires string data, but there is a set of string values that you can use and is defaulted to "r."

The buffer size parameter requires an integer and is defaulted to 0.

To practice using the open() function, create a file with the name sampleFile.txt inside your Python directory.

Try this sample code:

```
>>> file1 = open("sampleFile.txt")
>>> _
```

Note that the file function returns a file object.

The statement in the example assigns the file object to variable file1.

The file object has multiple attributes, and three of them are:

- Name: this contains the name of the file.
- Mode: this contains the access mode you used to access the file.

- Closed: this returns False if the file has been opened and True if the file is closed. When you use the open() function, the file is set to open.

Now, access those attributes.

>>> file1 = open("sampleFile.txt")

>>> file1.name

'sampleFile.txt'

>>> file1.mode

'r'

>>> file1.closed

False

>>> _

Whenever you are finished with a file, close them using the close() method.

>>> file1 = open("sampleFile.txt")

>>> file1.closed

False

>>> file1.close()

```
>>> file1.closed
```

True

```
>>> _
```

Remember that closing the file does not delete the variable or object.

To reopen the file, just open and reassign the file object.

For example:

```
>>> file1 = open("sampleFile.txt")
>>> file1.close()
>>> file1 = open(file1.name)
>>> file1.closed
```

False

```
>>> _
```

Reading from a File

Before proceeding, open the sampleFile.txt in your text editor.

Type "Hello World" in it and save.

Go back to Python.

To read the contents of the file, use the read() method.

For example:

>>> file1 = open("sampleFile.txt")

>>> file1.read()

'Hello World'

>>> _

File Pointer

Whenever you access a file, Python sets the file pointer.

The file pointer is like your word processor's cursor.

Any operation on the file starts at where the file pointer is.

When you open a file, and when it is set to the default access mode, which is "r" (read-only), the file pointer is set at the beginning of the file.

To know the current position of the file pointer, you can use the tell() method.

For example:

>>> file1 = open("sampleFile.txt")

```
>>> file1.tell()

0

>>> _
```

Most of the actions you perform on the file move the file pointer.

For example:

```
>>> file1 = open("sampleFile.txt")

>>> file1.tell()

0

>>> file1.read()

'Hello World'

>>> file1.tell()

11

>>> file1.read()

''

>>> _
```

To move the file pointer to a position you desire, you can use the seek() function.

For example:

>>> file1 = open("sampleFile.txt")

>>> file1.tell()

0

>>> file1.read()

'Hello World'

>>> file1.tell()

11

>>> file1.seek(0)

0

>>> file1.read()

'Hello World'

>>> file1.seek(1)

1

>>> file1.read()

'ello World'

\>>> _

The seek() method has two parameters.

The first is offset, which sets the pointer's position depending on the second parameter.

Also, the argument for this parameter is required.

The second parameter is optional.

It is for whence, which dictates where the "seek" will start.

It is set to 0 by default.

- If set to 0, Python will set the pointer's position to the offset argument.

- If set to 1, Python will set the pointer's position relative or in addition to the current position of the pointer.

- If set to 2, Python will set the pointer's position relative or in addition to the file's end.

Note that the last two options require the access mode to have binary access.

If the access mode does not have binary access, the last two options will be useful to determine the current position of the pointer [seek(0, 1)] and the position at the end of the file [seek(0, 2)].

For example:

```
>>> file1 = open("sampleFile.txt")

>>> file1.tell()

0

>>> file1.seek(1)

1

>>> file1.seek(0, 1)

0

>>> file1.seek(0, 2)

11

>>> _
```

File Access Modes

To write to a file, you will need to know more about file access modes in Python.

There are three types of file operations: reading, writing and appending.

Reading allows you to access and copy any part of the file's content.

Writing allows you to overwrite a file's contents and create a new one.

Appending allows you to write on the file while keeping the other content intact.

There are two types of file access modes: string and binary.

String access allows you to access a file's content as if you are opening a text file.

Binary access allows you to access a file in its rawest form: binary.

In your sample file, accessing it using string access allows you to read the line "Hello World."

Accessing the file using binary access will let you read "Hello World" in binary, which will be b'Hello World'.

For example:

>>> x = open("sampleFile.txt", "rb")

```
>>> x.read()

b'Hello World'

>>> _
```

String access is useful for editing text files.

Binary access is useful for anything else, like pictures, compressed files, and executables. In this book, you will only be taught how to handle text files.

You can enter multiple values in the file access mode parameter of the open() function.

But you do not need to memorize the combination.

You just need to know the letter combinations.

Each letter and symbol stands for an access mode and operation.

For example:

- r = read-only—file pointer placed at the beginning
    - r+ = read and write
- a = append—file pointer placed at the end
    - a+ = read and append

- w = overwrite/create—file pointer set to 0 since you create the file

    o w+ = read and overwrite/create

- b = binary

By default, file access mode is set to string.

You need to add b to allow binary access.

For example: "rb"

Writing to a File

When writing to a file, you must always remember that Python overwrites and does not insert file.

For example:

\>>> x = open("sampleFile.txt", "r+")

\>>> x.read()

'Hello World'

\>>> x.tell(0)

0

\>>> x.write("text")

4

>>> x.tell()

4

>>> x.read()

'o World'

>>> x.seek(0)

0

>>> x.read()

'texto World'

>>> _

You might have expected that the resulting text will be "textHello World."

The write method of the file object replaces each character one by one, starting from the pointer's current position.

Practice Exercise

For practice, you need to perform the following tasks:

- Create a new file named test.txt.

- Write the entire practice exercise instructions on the file.

- Close the file and reopen it.

- Read the file and set the cursor back to 0.

- Close the file and open it using append access mode.

- Add a rewritten version of these instructions at the end of the file.

- Create a new file and put similar content to it by copying the contents of the test.txt file.

Summary

Working with files in Python is easy to understand but difficult to implement.

As you already saw, there are only a few things that you need to remember.

The hard part is when you are actually accessing the file.

Remember that the key things you should master are the access modes and the file pointer's management.

It is easy to get lost in a file that contains a thousand characters.

Aside from being versed with file operations, you should also supplement your learning with the functions and methods of the str class in Python.

Most of the time, you will be dealing with strings if you need to work on a file.

Do not worry about binary yet.

That is a different beast altogether, and you will only need to tame it when you are already adept at Python.

As a beginner, expect that you will not deal yet with binary files that often contain media information.

Anyway, the next lesson is an elaboration on the "try" and "except" statements.

You'll discover how to manage and handle errors and exceptions effectively.

Chapter 9. Object-Oriented Programming

Object-oriented programming (OOP) is a programming paradigm in which programs are modeled according to their properties and behaviors rather than functions and logic.

All these elements are then bundled into objects.

Let's say, for example, an object could be you or me in real life.

It could be a person with a valid name, age, birth date, occupation, and other data or **properties** in terms of programming languages.

Also, we have certain **behaviors**. We can walk, talk, work, sleep, jog, and others as well.

So, OOP allows us to program and model real-world elements and make them as realistic and meaningful as possible.

Each entity in the world can be modeled as a Python object which possesses some data and does some function (has some behavior).

What have we been doing till now?

It's the procedural programming paradigm.

It provides steps, functions, and code blocks that follow a sequential order of completing commands.

Let's take a look at the most basic concepts of OOP; **Classes.**

Classes and Objects

To model real-world objects in programming, we need a blueprint of these objects or a prototype on which these objects will be based on.

Classes are basically user-defined blueprints that state how an object should look, what attributes or properties its object should have, and what it should do (the behaviors).

Basically, we describe the general behavior each object of a class can have.

What are objects?

Objects are *instances* of a class that we work with in life and programs.

This process, making objects from classes, is called instantiation.

Let's take an example under consideration.

If you've ever come across a car, let's see what attributes it can have:

- The color
- Number of tires
- Model of the car
- Engine specifications and others

When we program our class called **Car,** these will act as the properties of our car.

Now, what does the car do?

It drives, honks, and performs other functions internally.

These are the **properties or methods** of our class **Car.**

See how every car performs these actions and has these properties; **Classes are general representations of real-world objects.**

Objects are the specific instances of these classes and have relevant data in them.

For example, a Ford Mustang will be different from an SUV and have massively different properties.

Both of them are individual objects from our class Car.

Writing Classes

Let's head back to our editor and code an example class with properties and behaviors.

Here's the code: (don't stress, I'll explain everything later)

```
class Car:

    '''Modelling a car'''

    def __init__(self, model, license):

        '''Initialize all attributes and properties '''

        self.model = model

        self.license = license

    def drive(self):

        print("Vroom vroom! The car drives!")

    def honk(self):

        print("HONK! HONK!")

fordMustang = Car("ford-8", "AX-2939")

SUV = Car("Honda", "MX-2101")
```

Now, on to the analysis of the code we just wrote.

An Explanation on Classes (Code Breakdown)

We begin by defining our class on line one using the **class** keyword and immediately following it is the name of the class.

Conventionally, we start the name of the class in uppercase letters.

In line 2, we define a **docstring.**

It is a simple statement that tells us more about what the class has to offer or what it does.

On line 4, we finally define a function since we know that functions are defined using the def keyword.

All functions defined in a class are called **methods** of that class.

The __**init**__ is a special method provided by Python for every class, which, upon the instantiation process, runs automatically (when you create a new object).

A question you might have: Why the underscores?

They are to help you understand that Python's default function, and it shouldn't conflict with your own special function names.

Now, it takes in three parameters in our case, but it can have as many parameters as you want.

The **self** parameter is necessary and should come before others.

What is self?

The self-keyword is a reference that helps objects refer to themselves anywhere in the class.

It allows objects to have individual access to all the properties and methods defined in the class and doesn't interfere with other objects.

The self keyword is automatically passed whenever an object is made, and all other parameters can be passed with it (optional, but if used in the class declaration, they must be provided).

Now, on line 6, we prefix each parameter with self.

This is so, each object of the class has its own attributes (specific to it) and can be used throughout the class for that object only.

Next, we define two other functions and pass the self parameter to it, which is necessary, so each object has access to its own methods.

This is it for our class; let's see what happens next.

Making an Instance: Objects

Out of the class's scope, we are finally using our class to make objects of it (or cars out of the class Car).

These are basically instructions for how our class should behave for a specific car.

We can make an object using this syntax:

 objectOfTheClass = nameOfClass('param1', 'param2', ...)

Let's see how we did it for our example:

 fordMustang = Car("ford-8", "AX-2939")

 SUV = Car("Honda", "MX-2101")

Simply, we ask Python to make a car whose model is something and the license is something else.

Again, we ask Python to make a different car with different data.

How does it work?

As soon as you instantiate an object and assign it, the interpreter runs the __init__ function and assigns self to the newly made object, and also associates the passed arguments to the parameters.

The init method then returns an object, and it is assigned to our variable fordMustang.

Now, let's use this object to see what attributes or properties our objects have.

Accessing Attributes and Methods

Try running the following code after instantiating your class:

print(fordMustang.model)

print(fordMustang.license)

It prints what we sent to it using the arguments in our class.

As they are associated with our object now, the self.model is used to send back the data to us.

Here's the output:

```
ford-8
AX-2939
```

If you ask for these attributes from the second object, the output will be what you sent with it.

Here's an example:

print(SUV.model)

print(SUV.license)

```
Honda
MX-2101
```

Now, if you want to access the methods, simply use the dot operator again and ask for the methods.

Here's how:

> print(fordMustang.honk())

And it outputs:

```
HONK! HONK!
None
```

'None' is actually the return statement which is executing and printing as well.

Let's write a new method and use an attribute to see different outputs for different objects: (Add to your class from the last example)

> def mileage(self):
>
> val = input("What is the mileage? ")
>
> print(self.model + " Mileage: " + val)

When you run this on a class, you will be prompted to enter a value since we use the **input() function.**

Enter the value and let's check the output:

```
print(fordMustang.mileage())
```

```
What is the mileage? 2200
ford-8 Mileage:  2200
None
```

Similarly, you can run this in the second class.

Let's take a look at some other concepts for Object-oriented programming next.

This chapter covers a little more advanced topics from object-oriented programming like inheritance, child classes, and others.

Also, we'll see how to import classes just like we imported modules.

Inheritance

In real-world situations, most objects have a relationship to other objects.

Similarly, if we program something which is a specialized version of a more general element, this programming concept is called **Inheritance,** where a child class grabs all properties and methods from the parent class and makes use of them, and adds something of its own.

The parent class is the class that is more general and has all the basic functions.

For example, if we wrote the code for a Car, it is pretty general.

If now, we wish to write a class for an electric car, it will inherit most of the properties and behaviors from the parent (Car) class and add more stuff of its own.

Let's take a look at child classes next.

Child Classes: Writing One

We'll model an electric car, a more specific form of our Car class.

Here's the code and let's analyze it afterwards:

```python
class Car:
    def __init__(self, model, license):
        self.model = model
        self.license = license
    def drive(self):
        print("Vroom vroom! The car drives!")
    def mileage(self):
        val = input("What is the mileage? ")
```

```
        print(self.model + " Mileage: " + val)

class ElectricCar(Car):

    def __init__(self, model, license):

        super().__init__(model, license)

teslaX = ElectricCar("Tesla", "AA-9323")

print(teslaX.mileage())

print(teslaX.model)
```

```
What is the mileage? 343
Tesla Mileage: 343
None
Tesla
```

Firstly, we write our child class and use the parenthesis to provide to it, the parent class (Car).

Next, we declare the __init__ function just like we did before and pass to it the parameters and the self keyword to refer to the object.

Next, something strange.

We use the **super()** function and use the method __init__ to refer to the **parent class's init method.**

This is done so a connection can be made between the parent class and the child class, and now, it can access all attributes and methods of the parent class.

Although it doesn't have any function of its own right now, it can definitely be added in later.

Next, we make an object of our new ElectricCar class and ask for the methods and attributes, which yield expected output since now a relationship is made between the **parent and child or super and subclass.**

If you decide to assign methods to the child class, remember, the parent class can't access them.

But, the child class can definitely (always) access the methods of the parent class.

Importing Classes

As your programs grow, so will the complexity, both in logic and file size.

It is always recommended to ship your classes as individual files and import them wherever they are required.

This is possible using the import statements we studied a while ago.

Here's how you can import the classes into another file and use them properly:

1. from car import Car

2. from car import ElectricCar

3. from car import Car, ElectricCar

4. from car import *

5. import car

Chapter 10. Real-World Examples of Python

One might argue that Python's era was just 2017 when it witnessed some great rise in popularity and growth across the world. However, according to statistics and data, the recent rise in Python's growth could not be ignored.

However, why do you think it will keep on attaining the rise in expansion and in size?

To answer the question, we dive into the market data and the scale of Python adoption and acquisition by corporations and companies around the world.

SO the reason behind the popularity of Python is one and simple.

It will be as popular and widely used five years from now as it was five years ago.

This is a big statement, and to prove this, we need to see in detail what makes Python so special for these developers and programmers.

Years ago, when Python came into the market, people believed it would be dead within months of inception. In face when Larry Wall, who is also the founder and brain behind programing language Perl, was delivering his third annual state of Pearl Opinion, he said that there are some programming languages out there in the market that are C++, Java, Perl, Visual Basics, Javascript and in the last Python.

Back then, the leading language for programming was C++, and Perl was the third number in the market.

Python had very low demand and was not included among the PLs that could grow.

However, in the years to follow, Python grew with tremendous speed and outshined Perl as well.

According to Stack Overflow, the visitor volume to question and enquire about Python increased more rapidly than Perl.

The following are the reasons behind the rise and super demand for Python among developers.

Data Science

This is one of the most adored languages among data scientists, unlike R and C++.

So the current era is the era of big data, and since Python supports large sets of libraries, the internet, and prototypes, Python is the best and fully suited language for the operations.

PyMySQL, PyBrain, and NumPy are the reason why Python is so extensively demanded.

In addition, integrations and programming are the things a programmer has to deal with in everyday life, and this is the reason behind the huge demand for Python as well because it provides easy integration even of existing apps or sites to other programming languages.

This makes it future-oriented and scalable.

Machine Learning

These days, in the industry, artificial intelligence, and machine learning have created a huge buzz with every industry investing in the areas to maximize their revenue and cut costs.

This is not really possible without the induction of Python.

It is actually an interpreted language, and its use makes it elucidated enough to be interpreted by machines and to be understood by the hardware.

The growth of ML has been on the rise in the last few years, and I think this is also one of the reasons why Python has witnessed a surge in its demand.

Applications in Web Development

According to data, Python is chosen by two out of three developers who, in the start, worked with OHO, and this is an achievement.

In the last couple of years, the rising trend of Python shows that it seems like the best alternative. It offers Flask and Django, which makes the process of web development easy and quick. Due to these reasons and features, leading tech giants like Google, Facebook, Instagram, etc., have been using it for a long time. Uber and Google use it for their algorithms.

In addition, it is super simple, and this is the reason why it is easy to work with and adaptable.

Automation

Software development applications are SCons, which is for build control, Roundup, and Trace, which are for bug tracking and project management.

For IDE integrated development environments, a Roster is used.

- The most important stuff related to Python is that it provides special applications for education.

- Its applications in business include Tryton, which is a 3-tier and advanced level application platform.

  Another management software called Odoocomes with a huge deal of business applications. This actually makes Python an all-rounder.

- We have Twisted Python for network programming, which provides a platform and framework for the network programming that is asynchronous.

  It has a simple socket interface.

- We all know that the gaming industry is evolving with great potential and the ability to create a replicated amount of revenue.

  Python's applications for gaming are very safe to use and have been pretty much and widely used.

  PyGame and PyKyra are bi-development frameworks for games.

  There is also a variety of 3D rendering options in the libraries.

- Moreover, we have applications that interest the developers to a huge extent and are used widely.

   We have console-based applications, applications for robotics, machine learning, web scraping and scripting, and whatnot.

These are the main reason why Python is the best fit in the industry from the point of view of a developer.

According to a report of myTectra, the jobs posted in Naukri from 2014 to 2017 have been monitored.

The trend of Python jobs is compared to the world's number one language showing different results.

Things We Can Do in Python

In this chapter, we will discuss many things that you can do in Python.

Some of the things we can do in Python include the comments, reading and writing, files and integers, strings, and variables.

After reading this book, we are sure that you will be able to create a program that will run effectively.

Due to the interactive and descriptive nature of Python, a beginner can handle many things using it.

Therefore, this chapter will discuss some aspects and comments in Python to help you get started.

You can make amazing codes in a short time using the Python programming language.

Comment

A comment in the Python programming starts with the # sign.

This continues until the programmer gets to the end of the line.

A good example is;

This is a comment

Print (hello, thanks for contacting us)

It instructs your computer to print "Hello, thanks for contacting us."

The Python interpreter ignores all the comments.

As a programmer, however, you should not leave a comment after every line.

You can put in a comment when you need to explain something.

Since Python does not support long comments, it is important to use short and descriptive comments to avoid them going across the lines.

Reading and Writing

You will realize that some program requests specific information or show the text on the screen.

Sometimes we start the program code by informing the readers about our programs.

To ease things for the other coders, it is important to give it a name or title that is simple and descriptive.

As a programmer, you can use a string literal that comprises the print function to get the right data.

String literal is a line of the text surrounded by the quotes.

They can be either double or single quotes.

Although the type of quotes a programmer use matters less, the programmer must end with the quotes that he/she has used at the beginning of the phrase.

You can command your computer to display a phrase or a word on the screen by just doing as discussed above.

Files

Apart from using the print function to obtain a string when printing on the screen, it can be used to write something onto the file.

First, you will have to open up the myfile.txt and write on it before assigning it the myfile, which is a variable.

Once you have completed the first step, you will have to assign "w" in the new line to tell the program that you will only write or make changes after the file has opened.

It is not mandatory to use the print function; use the right methods like the reading method.

The reading method is used to open specific files to help you read the available data. You can use this option to open a specific file.

Generally, the read method helps the programmers to read the contents into variable data, making it easy for them to open the program they would like to read.

Integers

Always make sure that the integers are kept as whole numbers if you are using them. They can be negative or positive only if there are no decimals. However, if your number has a decimal point, use it as a floating number.

Python will automatically display such integers on the screen.

Moreover, you cannot place one number next to others if you are using the integers because Python is a strongly typed language; thus, it will not recognize them when you use them together.

However, you put both the number and the string together by making sure you turn the number into a string first before going to the next steps.

Triple Quotes

After reading and understanding both the single and double quotes, it is now time to look at the triple quotes.

The triple quotes are used to define the literal that spans many lines.

You can use three singles, double, or single when defining an authentic.

Strings

Although a string is seen as a complicated thing to many beginners, it is a term used by the programmers when referring to a sequence of characters and works just like a list.

A string contains more functionality, which is specific than a list.

You will find it challenging to format the strings when writing out the code because some messages will not be fixed easily due to its functionality.

String formatting is the only way to go away within such a situation.

Escape Sequences

They are used to donate special characters that are hard to type on the keyboard or those that can be reserved to avoid confusion that may occur in programming.

Operator Precedence

It will help you to track what you are doing in Python.

It makes things easy when ordering the operation to receive the right information.

So, take enough time to understand how the operator precedence works to avoid confusion.

Variables

Variables refer to the labels donated somewhere in the computer memory to store something like holding values and numbers.

In the programming typed statistically, the variables have predetermined values.

However, Python enables you to use one variable to store many different types.

For example, in the calculator, variables are like memory function to hold values that can be retrieved if you need them later.

The variables can only be erased if you store them in the newer value.

You will have to name the variable and ensure it has an integer value.

Moreover, the programmer can define a variable in Python by providing the label value.

For instance, a programmer can name a variable count and even make it an integer of one, and this can be written as; count=1.

It allows you to assign the same name to the variable, and in fact, the Python interpreter cannot read through the information if you are trying to access values in the undefined variable.

It will display a message showing syntax error.

Also, Python provides you with the opportunity of defining different variables in one line, even though this not good according to our experience.

The Scope of a Variable

It is not easy to access everything in Python, and there will be differences in the length of the variables.

However, the way we define the variable plays a vital role in determining the location and the duration of accessing the variables.

The part of the program that allows you to access the variable is called the Scope, while the time taken for accessing the variable is a lifetime.

Global variables refer to the variables defined in the primary file body.

These variables are visible throughout the file and also in the file that imports specific data.

As such, these variables cause a long-term impact, which you may notice when working on your program.

This is the reason why it is not good to use global variables in the Python program.

We advise programmers to add stuff into the global namespace only if they plan to use them internationally.

A local variable is a variable defined within another variable.

You can access local variables from the region they are assigned.

Also, the variables are available in the specific parts of the program.

Modifying Values

It is easy for an individual to define a particular variable whose values have been set for many programming languages. The values, which cannot be modified or changed in the programming language, are called constants.

Although this kind of restriction is not allowed in Python, there are used to ensure some variables are marked, indicating that no one should change those values.

You must write the name in capital letters, separated with underscores.

A good example is shown below:

NUMBER_OF_HOURS_IN_A_DAY=24

It is not mandatory to put the correct number in the end.

Since Python programming does not keep tracking and has no rules for inserting the correct value in the end, you are free and allowed to say, for example, that they are 25 hours in a day.

However, it is important to put the correct value for other coders to use in case they want.

Modifying values is essential in your string as it allows a programmer to change the maximum number in the future.

Therefore, understanding the working of the string in the program contributes a lot to your program's success.

One has to learn and know where to store the values, the rules governing each value, and how to make them perform well in a specific area.

The Assignment Operator

It refers to an equal sign (=).

You will be using the assignment operator to assign values to the variable located at the left side on the statement's right.

However, you must evaluate if the value on the right side is an arithmetic expression.

Note that the assignment operator is not a mathematical sign in the programming because, in programming, we are allowed to add all types of things and make them look like they are equivalent to a certain number.

This sign is used to show that those items can be changed or turned into the part on the other side.

Chapter 11. Getting Started; Python Tips and Tricks

We have spent the last few days of this guidebook looking at some of the different parts of the Python language that we can work with.

These are meant to help us get going with some of our coding in Python and will ensure that we can write some of your codes in no time.

With some of this information in mind, we can work on some of the final skills that we need to focus on before we are done.

We are going to look at some of the tips and tricks that will help you to get started with Python, along with how we can work with web scraping and debugging some of our programs as well.

Let's get started with this one to help us get started and finalize how good our codes can be.

Web Scraping

Imagine for a moment that we are going to pull up a large amount of data from many websites, and we want to be able to do this at a very fast rate.

How would we be able to go through this without having to go manually through each of the websites that we have and gathering the data in this manner?

This is where the process of web scraping is going to come into play.

Companies will use web scraping to collect a large amount of information from websites.

But why does someone want to go through and collect all of this data, in such large amounts, from these websites in the first place?

There are a lot of reasons for this, and some of them are going to include the following:

- *Price comparison:* some of the different services that are out there, such as ParseHub, will work with this process in order to collect data from websites for online shopping and then can use this in order to compare prices of similar products.

- *Email address gathering:* we can use the process of web scraping in order to help with marketing.

    This can help us to collect the email IDs that come with customers and then send out bulk emails to these individuals as well.

- *Social media scraping:* web scraping is going to be used to collect data from social media sites and then figure out what is trending.

- *Research and development:* web scraping is going to be used to help a company collect a lot of data from websites.

  We can then analyze this and use it to finish our surveys and to help out with research and development.

- *Job listing:* details regarding openings of jobs, interviews, and more can be collected from a variety of websites, and then we can list them in one place in order to make them easier for the user to access

Web scraping is going to be more of an automated method that we can use in order to get a huge amount of data from any website that we choose.

The data that we are able to get out of these websites will be unstructured.

And this web scraping helps a company to collect all of this data and then will ensure that they are able to store it in a structured form.

There are a variety of methods that we are able to use in order to scrape these websites that we want, including online Services, writing out some of your own codes, and APIs.

Talking about whether or not scraping of this kind is seen as legal or not, it can depend on what the website says.

Some websites are fine with this, and some are not.

You can check with each website to figure out whether they are fine with it, and if they are, you are able to continue with your web scraping tools and gather up the information that you need.

Since we are talking about Python here, we are going to take some time to see how we are able to use Python to help out with web scraping.

But this brings up the reasons why we would want to work with Python to help out with this process rather than working with some of the other coding languages that are out there. Some of the features that come with Python and can make it more suitable for web scraping will include:

- *It is easy to use:* the code that you are able to use along with Python is going to be simple.

    This ensures that any of the codes that you want to use for web scraping will not be as messy to work with and can be easy to use.

- *A large library collection:* There are a lot of libraries that work with data science and web scraping that are also compatible with what the Python language is able to do.

  These include options like Pandas, Matplotlib, and NumPy.

  This is why you will find that the Python language is going to be suitable for web scraping and even for some of the other manipulations that you want to do with the extracted data.

- *Dynamically typed:* this is something in Python where you will not need to go through and define all of the types of data that you are using with our variables.

  Instead, you are able just to use these variables wherever you would like.

  This is going to save a lot of time when it comes to working on the codes and can make your job faster than ever.

- The syntax of Python is going to be easy to understand the syntax that we are able to see with Python is easy to understand, mainly because the statements that come with this are going to be written in English.

It is going to be expressive and easy to read, and the indentations will make it easier for us to figure out between the different parts of the code.

- A small line of code is able to handle some large tasks.

    Web scraping is a process that we are going to use in order to save some time.

    And with Python, you can write out a small amount of code to get some of the big tasks that you would like to accomplish.

    This is going to save you time not only when it comes to figuring out the important data that comes in that website, but can also help you to save time when you would like to write out the codes.

- *Community:* at times, when you are a beginner, you are going to find that there are parts of the code that are hard to work with and are not going to go as smoothly as you had hoped in the process.

    This is where you will find the Python language to be healthy.

If you get stuck while writing out some of your code, you will like that the Python community is going to help you to answer your questions and get things done on the code in no time.

Now that we know some of the benefits that come with Python, especially the ones that are going to help us to handle some of the web scrapings that we want to do, it is time for us to take things to the next step and look at how the process of web scraping is going to work.

When you run out the code that you want to work within web scraping, you will find that there is a request that is sent out to the URL.

Then there is going to be a response sent back from that request, and then the server is able to send the data and allows you a chance to read the page, whether it is XML or HTML at the time.

The code is then able to go through and parse the XML or HTML page, find the data, and takes it out.

The location where you are going to find this data when it is extracted will depend on what you told the code to do.

Often it is going to be moved over to a database so that you are able to search through it later and learn more from it as well.

There are going to be a few simple steps that you are able to take to make something to help us go through the process of extracting the data with the help of web scraping in Python.

The steps that will help you to use Python to help with web scraping will include:

- Find the URL that you would like to scrape in the first place.

- Inspect the page that you are planning on using.

- Find the data that is on the page that you would like to extract.

- Write out the code that you would like to use with the help of Python in order to complete this process.

- Run the code that you just wrote and then extract out the data that you would like to use.

- Store the data in the format that would be the most helpful for you in the process.

There are also a few options that you are able to use when it is time to work on the process of web scraping.

As we know, Python is already able to be used for a lot of different types of applications, and there are going to be a ton of libraries with Python that is going to be used for different purposes.

There are a few libraries that work the best when it comes to working with the process of data web scraping will include:

1. *Selenium:* this is going to be a web testing library.

   It is going to be used to help automate some of the activities that are found on your browser.

2. *BeautifulSoup:* this is going to be one of those packages that you are able to use with Python to help us to parse HTML and XML documents.

   It is also able to create parse trees that can help us to extract the data in an easy manner.

3. *Pandas:* this is one of the best libraries to rely on when it is time to handle any kind of work that you would like in data analysis and data science.

   Pandas are often going to be used to help out with any of the data analysis and the data manipulation that you would like.

   When it comes to web scraping, you will find that Pandas is going to be used in order to extract the data and then get it stored in the right format in the way that you would like along the way.

There are many times when a company is going to try and gather up data from other websites and from many other sources.

This is one of the first steps that is going to be found when we are working with data analysis and using that information to improve a business through their customers, the industry, or from the other competition out there.

But going through and manually gathering all of that data is going to take too long and can be really hard to work with as well.

With the large amounts of data that are being used and generated on a daily basis, it is no wonder that so many companies are working with processes like web scraping to handle all of the work in a timely manner as well.

When we work with web scraping and do some of the codings that are necessary with the help of Python, we will find that we are able to get through the information in a fast manner and get it stored in the right place for our needs, without having to do all of the work manually.

This can make the process of data analysis much easier overall and will ensure that we are able to see some of the results that we want with this as well.

And with some of the right Python algorithms and codes, we can get data scraping done in no time.

Chapter 12. Common Programming Challenges

The excitement about programming can fizzle out fast and turn into a nightmare.

There are unexpected challenges that might make life difficult for you, especially as a beginner programmer. However, these challenges should not set you back or kill your resolve.

They are common challenges that a lot of people have experienced before, and they overcame them, as you will too.

If you want to succeed in programming, you should be aware of the fact that mistakes do happen, and you will probably make many of them.

The downside of mistakes is that you can feel you are not good enough.

Everyone else seems to be doing fine, but not you.

On the flip side, mistakes are an opportunity for you to learn and advance.

No one was born as good as they are today.

What we are is the sum of mistakes and learning from those mistakes and experiences.

Feel free to reach out to mentors whenever you feel stuck.

Deadlines and bug reports might overwhelm you, but once you get the hang of it, you will do great.

The following are some common challenges that you might experience as a beginner programmer.

Debugging

You feel content with a project, satisfied that it will run without a hitch and perform the desired duties.

However, when you arrive at your desk in the morning, your quality assurance team has other ideas.

They point out what seems like endless issues with the project.

Perhaps the *OK* button is not responsive; the error messages are not displaying correctly, and so forth.

All these are issues that eventually leave a negative impact on the user experience.

You must get back to the drawing board and figure out where the problem lies.

Debugging will be part of your life as a programmer.

It is not enjoyable, but it is reality.

Debugging is one of the most exhausting things you have to do.

If you are lucky, you will encounter bugs that can be fixed easily.

Debugging costs you hours and lots of coffee.

However, you should not feel downtrodden yet.

Bugs are all over the place in programming.

Even the best code you will ever come across needs debugging at some point.

Solution

How do you handle the debugging process and make your life easier?

The first step is to document your work.

Documentation might seem like a lot of work for you, but it helps you trace your steps in the event of an error.

That way, you can easily trace the source and fix it, saving you from inspecting hundreds or thousands of code.

Another way of doing light work of debugging is to recreate the problem.

You must understand what the problem is before you try to solve it.

If you recreate the problem, you isolate it from the rest of the code and get a better perspective of it.

Talk to someone.

You might not always have all the answers.

Do not fear anyone, especially if you work in a team.

Beginner programmers often feel some people are out of reach, perhaps because of the positions they hold.

However, if you do not ask for help, you will never really know whether the person will be helpful or not.

The best person to ask for help, for example, is the quality tester who identified the problem, especially if you are unable to recreate the problem.

Working Smart

As a programmer, one thing you must be aware of is that you will be sitting down for hours on end working on some code.

This becomes your normal routine.

However, you are aware of the risks this poses to your health. Neck sprains, numb legs, back pain, pain in your palms and fingers from typing away all day.

For a beginner, you might not be ready for the challenge yet.

However, you must still dig in daily to meet your deliverables.

Solution

The first thing you must consider is regular exercise.

If you work a desk job, it is possible to lose motivation and feel exhausted even before your workday is over.

You can tackle this by keeping a workout routine.

Jog before you go to work every morning, take a brisk half-hour walk, and so forth.

There are many simple routines that you can initiate, which will help you handle the situation better.

While at work, take some time off and walk around—without looking like you are wasting time.

This helps to relieve your body of the pain and pressure, and more importantly, allows for proper blood circulation.

Other than that, you do not have to keep typing while seated.

Stand up from time to time.

Some companies have invested in height-adjustable desks, which help with this.

User Experience

One of the most common challenges you will experience as a programmer is managing user experiences.

You will come across a lot of clients in the course of your programming career.

However, not all clients know how to communicate their needs.

As a result, you will be involved in a lot of back and forth on project details and deliverables.

Most users have a good idea of what they need the project you are developing to do.

However, this is not always the same as what your development team believes.

Given that most beginner programmers never interact directly with the clients, it might be difficult for you to understand them, especially in a team project.

Solution

The best way around this is to figure out the best features of the project.

Your client already knows what they want the project to do.

Ask the right questions, especially to your team members who are in direct contact with the client or the end-user.

The best responses will often come from designers and user experience experts.

Their insight comes from interacting with users most of the time.

Another option is to test the product you are designing.

You have probably used test versions of some products in the past.

Most major players in the tech industry release beta versions of their products before the final.

This way, users try it out, share their views, ideas, and challenges they encounter.

This information is collected and used to refine the beta product before the final one is released.

Testing your product allows you to identify and fix bugs before you release the product to the end-user.

It also allows you to interact with the user and gauge the level of acceptance for your project.

Estimates

A lot of beginner programmers struggle with scheduling.

Perhaps you gave an estimate for a task and you are unable to meet it.

You are now a professional.

Never delude yourself that you are not, perhaps because you are a beginner.

This industry focuses on deadlines a lot.

In software development, estimates are crucial.

They are often used to plan bigger schedules for projects, and in some cases, agree on the project quotes.

Delays end up in problems that might, in the long run, affect trust between the parties involved.

Solution

The first step towards getting your estimates right is to apportion time properly.

Time management is key.

Set out a schedule within which you can complete a given task.

Within that schedule, allow yourself ample buffer time for any inconvenience, but not too much time.

For example, allow yourself 30-40 minutes for an assignment that should take 20 minutes.

Another way of improving your scheduling challenges is to break down assignments into micro milestones.

A series of small tasks is easier to manage.

Besides, when you complete these micro assignments, you are more psyched about getting onto the next one, and so on.

You end up with a lighter workload, which is also a good way to prevent burnout.

Constant Updates

The tech industry keeps expanding in leaps and bounds.

You can barely go a month before you learn about some groundbreaking work.

Everything keeps upgrading or updating to better, more efficient versions. Libraries, tools, and frameworks are not left behind, either.

Updates are awesome.

Most updates improve user experiences and bolster the platform security.

However, updates come with undue pressure, even for the most experienced programmers out there.

Solution

Stay abreast of the latest developments in your field of expertise.

You cannot know everything, but catching up on trends from time to time will help you learn some new tools and tips available, which can also help you improve your skills and develop cutting edge products.

Another option is to learn.

The beauty of the world of IT is that things are always changing.

It is one of the most dynamic industries today.

Carve out half an hour daily to learn something new.

You will be intrigued by how much you will have mastered after a few weeks.

In your spare time, challenge yourself to build something simple, solve a problem, and so forth.

There are lots of challenge websites available today where you can have a go at real-world problems.

Problems Communicating

Beginner programmers face communication challenges all the time.

You are new to the workplace, so you do not really know anyone.

Most of the team members and managers are alien to you, and as a result, you often feel out of place. At some point in time, every programmer goes through this.

You feel like a baby among giants.

Eventually, the pressure gets to you, and you make a grave mistake, which could have been avoided if you reached out to someone to assist.

Solution

Dealing with communication problems is more than just a social interaction concern.

First, you must learn to be proactive.

If something bugs you, ask for help.

The worst that can happen is people might laugh, especially if it is a rookie question, but someone will go out of their way and help you.

If they don't and something goes awry, the department shoulders the blame for their ignorance.

Before you know it, people will keep checking in on you to make sure you are getting it right, and you might also make some good friends in the process.

Consistency is another way to handle the communication challenge.

For a beginner, you might not always get everything right.

These are moments you can learn from.

With practice, you grow bolder and learn to express yourself better over time.

Security Concerns

Data is the new gold.

This is the reality of the world right now.

Data is precious and is one of the reasons why tech giants are facing lawsuits all over the place.

Huawei recently found itself in a spat with the US government that ended up in a host of severed ties.

There are so many reasons behind the US government's hard stance against Huawei, and most of them circle back to data.

People are willing to pay a great deal of money to access specific data that can benefit them in one way or the other.

Some companies play the short-term game; others are in it for the long-term.

Competitors also use nefarious ways to gain access to their competitors' databases and see what they are working on and how they do it.

As a programmer, one thing your clients expect from you is that their data is safe, and the data their clients share with them through your project.

Beginner programmers are fairly aware of all the security risks involved.

This should not worry you so much, especially if you are part of a team of able developers.

They will always have contingency measures in place.

However, you must not be ignorant of security loopholes, especially in your code.

Solution

Hackers are always trying to gain access to some code.

You cannot stop them from trying.

However, you can make it difficult for them to penetrate your code.

Give them a challenge.

The single biggest threat to any secure platform is human interaction.

At times, someone will not compromise your code from outside but someone you know.

In most cases, they compromise your code without knowing they do—unless they did it intentionally.

Make sure your workstation is safe.

Every time you step away from your workstation, ensure your screen is locked, and if you are going away for a long time, shut down your devices.

It is also advisable in your programming language that you use parameterized queries, especially for SQL injections.

This is important because most hackers use SQL injections to gain access and steal information.

Relying on Foreign Code

You have written some code for a few years and believe in your ability.

You are confident you are good enough, hence being hired by the company.

However, make peace with the fact that you will have to work on projects that were written by someone else.

Working with another person's code is not always an easy thing, especially if their code seems outdated.

There is a reason why the company insists on using that particular code.

The worst possible situation would be company politics–they occur everywhere.

Someone wrote some code that the entire company relies on, but you cannot change or question it because the original coder connects with the company hierarchy.

Often this raises a problem where you are unable to figure out the code.

Solution

Since there is not much you can do about the code, why not try to learn it?

If you can, talk to the developer who wrote it and understand their reasoning behind it.

This way, it is easier for you to embrace their style, and you will also have a smooth time handling your projects.

You never know; you might just show them something new and help them rethink their code.

Another option is to embrace this code.

It is not yours, but it is what you have and will be using for a very long time.

Change your attitude about that code.

Take responsibility for the code and work with it.

This way, your hesitation will slowly fade away.

Lack of Planning

While you have a burning desire to impress in your new place of work, you must have a plan.

Many beginner programmers do not.

Many programmers jump into writing code before stopping in their tracks to determine the direction they want to steer the code.

The problem with this approach is that you will fail to make sense.

The code might sound right in your head, but on paper, nothing works.

Solution

Conceptualize an idea.

Everything starts with an idea.

Say you want to write a program that allows users to share important calendar dates and milestones with their loved ones.

Focusing on this idea helps you remember why you are writing that code.

Once you have an idea, how do you connect it with real problems?

What are the problems you are trying to solve?

How are they connected to your idea?

This also begs the question—why do people need your program?

Planning will help you save time when writing a program, and at the same time, help you stay on track.

Finally

In programming, everyone starts somewhere.

Being the new person in the company should not scare you.

Communicate with your peers and seniors, be willing to learn from them, and all the things that might seem overwhelming will somehow become easier as time goes by.

Conclusion

Programming is not easy. In fact, it's rather difficult, and there are topics that are sadly too esoteric to cover in this book.

For example, we didn't get to the bulk of file operations, nor did we get to things like object-oriented programming.

But I hope what I've given you is a very solid foundational understanding of Python so that you can get ready to learn about these things.

Python—It is a language named after Monty Python.

It is a programming language that has taken the world by storm.

The applications we have seen so far, the examples we have discovered, and the future prospects of the language, when combined, point out one thing for sure.

If you are a programmer, Python is your ticket to the future.

When learning a new language, there will always be challenges.

There will be times where you might even be frustrated and call it a day.

The thing to remember here is this: many others have gone through this road just like you.

Some have gone on to become successful, while others have remained within the shadow of someone else.

It is up to you to grab the opportunity and become a unique and different programmer, and learning Python is just a part of the journey.

Through Python, you will be able to do so much more than just design 2D snake games.

Python has paved the way for many success stories and has certainly become the most popular language.

Now you know why!

It is time for you to add Python to your resume and deliver results in the most effective and efficient manner possible.

Good luck, and have a great programming journey ahead!

I am not going to hold your hand.

But what I can say is that you have worked hard to be a programmer, and you have worked hard throughout the course of this book, likewise.

Not all of the concepts within this book are easy to understand, even with more in-depth explanations.

My goal here wasn't explicitly to teach you Python or object-oriented programming or any of that: my goal was to teach you the computer.

The way it thinks, and the way programs are written.

Anybody can learn Python keywords.

But to learn to program and to write effective solid code regardless of which programming language that you're using, that's another skill entirely.

Now that you have finished this book, you should be able to do a lot of programs for different situations.

The next step is to keep practicing a lot in order to become a master of Python.

While programming, sometimes you might think that some things are impossible to code or that you are not good enough to do them.

But that is not right; you just have to think a lot in order to make it happen.

Also, while programming, you may find that your code or program is not working, do not worry. Even the smartest people write codes that do not work at the beginning.

You just have to keep trying.

As you know, nowadays technology is everywhere, and so programming. Our recommendation is that you should try to code and solve problems of your daily activities in order to broaden your vision of the world since all electronics have hundreds and hundreds of lines of codes on them.

I sincerely hope that this book has helped you to get on the road to accomplishing everything that you want to accomplish in the world of programming.

Remember going forward that without a doubt, it will not always be easy.

It won't be even remotely easy.

Programming is made difficult by its very nature.

Humans, we just don't think like computers.

But hopefully, I've helped you to understand programming, at least.

www.ingramcontent.com/pod-product-compliance
Lightning Source LLC
Chambersburg PA
CBHW071353210526
45465CB00001B/67